Key Geography for GCSE

David Waugh

Former Head of Geography
Trinity School
Carlisle

Book 1

Stanley Thornes (Publishers) Ltd

First published in 1994 and reprinted eight times.

Second edition published in 1998 by:
Stanley Thornes (Publishers) Ltd
Ellenborough House
Wellington Street
CHELTENHAM GL50 1YW
England

98 99 00 01 02 / 10 9 8 7 6 5 4 3 2 1

A catalogue record for this book is available from the British Library.

First edition ISBN 0 7487 1670 X
Second edition ISBN 0 7487 3603 4

Printed and bound in Italy by
STIGE, Turin

Acknowledgements

The author and publishers are grateful to the following for permission to reproduce photographs and other copyright material in this book.

Aerofilms Ltd 9F, 27C, 30C, 94B, 161C; Chris Bentley 122B; Penni Bickle 113C, D; Blenkinsop Studios 139B; Sue Bolton 126B; British Petroleum plc 108C; J. Allan Cash Ltd 10B, 45F, 112A, 161D, 165D; John Chandler/Kea Graphics 167D; Bruce Coleman Ltd 120A; Robin Cousins 145E; Cumbrian Library Service, Kendal 154A; Prodeepta Das 93E; Eye Ubiquitous 11D, 29E, 33D, 57 C, 93D, 147C; Forest Life Picture Library 152B; Frank Lane Picture Agency 120A, 123D; Geoscience Features 144C; Greenpeace 36A; Getty Images 29C, 59C, D; Hutchison Library 79E, 111F (left); ICCe Photo Library 124B, 127D, 129D, 135C, 142A (bottom), 143 (bottom), 153C; ICI Chemicals and Polymers Ltd 172D; Impact Photos 159C; Intermediate Technology 143 (top); Harry Keys/Karen Williams 166A, B, 167C; Landforms 24B(b), 25C, 39F, 40B, 41F, 44B; Mary Evans Picture Library 98B; Meadowhall Centre Ltd 148B; Newcastle Football Club 103D; North News and Pictures 157D; Nuclear Electric 133B; Panos Pictures 74A, 93C, 108B; Planet Earth Pictures 51C, 165D; Press Association 170D; Rex

Features/Sipa Press 57C, 78A, 91E, F, 101C, 165E; Robert Harding Picture Library 74B, 77D, 79D, 90A, 97D, 98C, 108A, 111F, 138A (top); Science Photo Library (i), 8A, 29F, 34C, 44C, 48A, 50A, 51E, 64A; Scottish Hydro-Electric 133C; Sefton Picture Library 97C, 144D, 147C; Spectrum Picture Library 97F; Still Pictures 131C; Syndication International 29D, 146A; Telegraph Colour Library 19D; Tony Stone Images cover, 4C, 7F, 34B, 61C, 63B, 75C, 77C, 90B, 96B, 97G, 107C, 126C; Topham Picturepoint 56A, 120A, 126A, 152B, 154C, 158A; Tower Hamlets Local History Library 99C; Toyota Motor Manufacturing (UK) Ltd 169D, 171C; Trip Photographic Library 113B, 160B, 173C, 174B, C; University of Cambridge 138A; Dr A. C. Waltham 16A, 22B, 25D, 41E, 42A, 46D, 49E; Simon Warner 42A, 46A, B, C, 123C, 124C, 145F, 152B (left), 156A; David Waugh 4B, 6D, 10C, 63C, 87E, F, G, 97E, 100B, 103C (top and bottom), 109C (both), 142A (top), 150B, 151D, E, 158B, 159D; Eric Whitehead 154D; Mike Williams 152B (top right), 157C; Woodfall Wild Images 5E, 17D, 110C; World Pictures 23E, 30A, 40C, 150C.

Figure D, page 115 – the by-pass route is reproduced courtesy of the Department of Transport; figure D, page 33 – adapted extract from 'The Ganges' by Tim McGirk, reproduced

from The Independent on Sunday, 9 August 1992; figure D, page 149 – the floorplan is reproduced courtesy of the Meadowhall Centre Ltd, Sheffield; figure B, page 114 – map extract from Philip's Modern School Atlas (91st edition) © George Philip.

The map extracts on pages 43, 47, 82–83 and 115 are reproduced from the 1995 Ordnance Survey map of Snowdonia (Landranger 115), the 1994 Ordnance Survey map of Wensleydale and Upper Wharfedale (Landranger 98), the 1995 Ordnance Survey map of Carlisle and Solway Firth (Landranger 85) and the 1991 Ordnance Survey map of Haltwhistle, Bewcastle and Alston (Landranger 86). Maps reproduced from the Ordnance Survey Landranger mapping with permission of The Controller of Her Majesty's Stationery Office © Crown copyright; Licence number 07000U.

The author also wishes to thank Gilbert Hitchen for his contribution to pages 122–124.

Every effort has been made to contact copyright holders and we apologise if any have been overlooked.

Contents

Landforms and natural hazards

1 Rivers – river basins, processes, landforms, flooding *4*
2 Coasts – processes, landforms, flooding *22*
3 Water pollution – rivers, lakes, seas *32*
4 Glaciation, limestone, rock structure *38*
5 Earthquakes and volcanoes *50*

Human geography

6 Population – distribution and trends, causes of migration *62*
7 Settlement – types, sites and urban growth *80*
8 Urban patterns and changes *94*
9 Transport – types, problems (including pollution) and solutions *104*

Economic geography

10 Employment structures *116*
11 Primary activities – farming, energy resources, the environment *120*
12 Secondary activities *136*
13 Tertiary (service) activities – shops and offices (location and hierarchy); tourism and the need to plan and manage certain environments *144*

Case Studies

A Coastal management – part of the Wessex coast *160*
B A volcanic eruption – Ruapehu, New Zealand *164*
C A transnational car company – Toyota *168*
D The cycle of industrial change – Teesside *172*

Index *176*

What are the main features of a river basin?

A **river** (or **drainage**) **basin** is an area of land drained by a river and its tributaries. The higher land which forms the boundary of the river basin, and which separates two river basins, is called the **watershed**. Most rain falls in mountainous areas. Rain falling on higher land near the watershed will flow slowly downhill either over the surface (photo **A**) or through any topsoil. In time the water will collect in a channel to form a small stream which, as it continues downhill, will increase in size to become a river.

A The watershed of a river basin above its source in the Pennines. Rainfall is flowing over the land surface, but the water has yet to make a channel for itself.

Source of main river

Photo A

Watershed

Photo B

Steep valley sides

No valley floor

B The River Glasyn flowing through a steep-sided valley in Snowdonia

Watershed

Tributary

Confluence
Photo C

The confluence of the Amazon (reddish water) and the Rio Negro (black water). The waters are different densities and do not mix for about 50 km. **C**

The point at which a river begins is called its **source**. At first the channel is small but it increases rapidly as the river is joined by many **tributaries**. A tributary is a small stream or river flowing into the main river. The place where a tributary joins the main river is its **confluence**. The river valley, in highland areas, is usually steep-sided (photo **B**). As the river approaches lower land, its valley sides become less steep and its channel widens (photo **C**). Most rivers eventually flow into the sea, although a few end in lakes. The end of a river is known as its **mouth** (photo **E**).

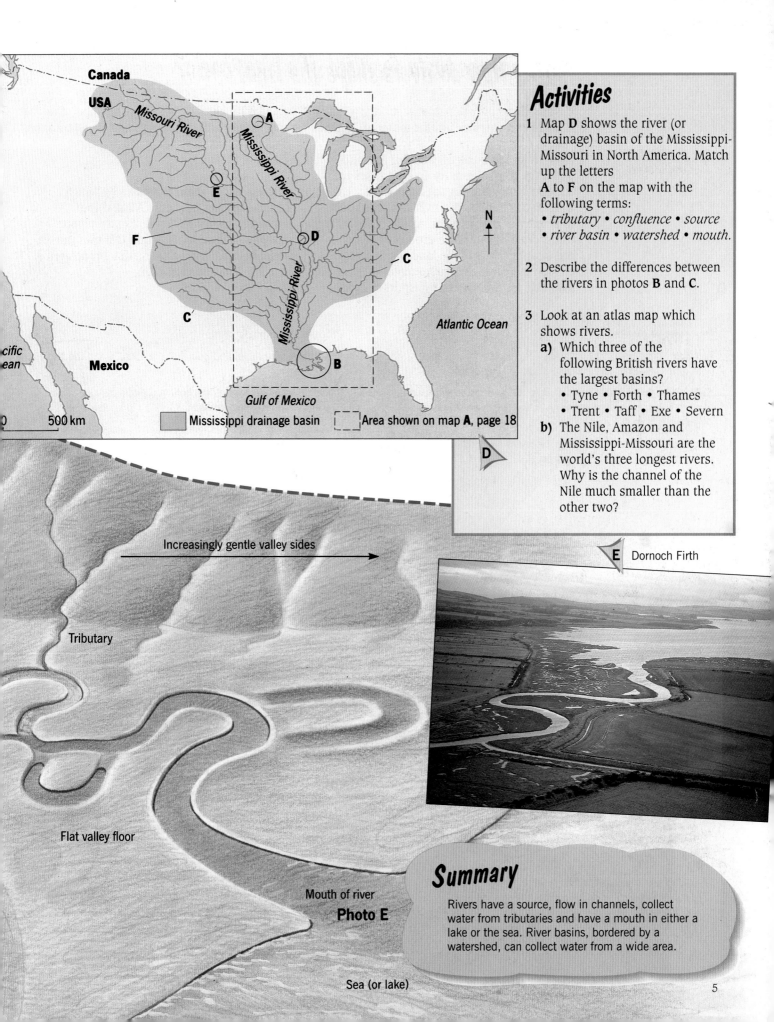

Canada

USA

Missouri River

Mississippi River

E

F

D

C

C'

B

Mexico

cific
ean

Pacific Ocean

Atlantic Ocean

N

Mississippi River

Gulf of Mexico

0   500 km

Mississippi drainage basin

Area shown on map **A**, page 18

D

Activities

1 Map **D** shows the river (or
   drainage) basin of the Mississippi-
   Missouri in North America. Match
   up the letters
   A to **F** on the map with the
   following terms:
   • *tributary* • *confluence* • *source*
   • *river basin* • *watershed* • *mouth*.

2 Describe the differences between
   the rivers in photos **B** and **C**.

3 Look at an atlas map which
   shows rivers.
   a) Which three of the
      following British rivers have
      the largest basins?
      • Tyne • Forth • Thames
      • Trent • Taff • Exe • Severn
   b) The Nile, Amazon and
      Mississippi-Missouri are the
      world's three longest rivers.
      Why is the channel of the
      Nile much smaller than the
      other two?

E Dornoch Firth

Increasingly gentle valley sides

Tributary

Flat valley floor

Mouth of river

Photo E

Sea (or lake)

Summary

Rivers have a source, flow in channels, collect
water from tributaries and have a mouth in either a
lake or the sea. River basins, bordered by a
watershed, can collect water from a wide area.

How do rivers shape the land?

If water flows over the ground surface (photo **A**, page 4) it can pick up fine material. Where valleys have very steep sides (photo **B**, page 4), large rocks can break off and fall downhill under the force of gravity. In both cases the material can end up in the channel of a river. Once in its channel, the river can **transport** this material downstream. As the material is transported, it can cause **erosion**. Erosion is the wearing away of the land. As the rate of erosion increases then more material becomes available for the river to transport. A cycle is created in which erosion depends upon the river transporting material, and transportation depends upon the river producing more material by erosion.

There are four main processes by which a river can cause erosion (figure **A**), and four processes by which a river can transport material (figure **B**). Diagram **C** shows the relationship between the various processes of erosion and transportation.

A

Processes of erosion

Attrition – material is moved along the bed of a river, collides with other material, and breaks up into smaller pieces.

Corrasion – fine material rubs against the river bank. The bank is worn away, by a sand-papering action called abrasion, and collapses (photo **D**).

Corrosion – some rocks forming the banks and bed of a river are dissolved by acids in the water.

Hydraulic action – the sheer force of water hitting the banks of the river.

B

Processes of transportation

Traction – large rocks and boulders are rolled along the bed of the river.

Saltation – smaller stones are bounced along the bed of a river in a leap-frogging motion.

Suspension – fine material, light enough in weight to be carried by the river. It is this material that discolours the water.

Solution – dissolved material is transported by the river.

C

River bank

Fine, light material held in suspension (**transport**) rubs against bank, wearing it away (**erosion**)

Dissolved material (**erosion**) carried along in solution (**transport**)

Large boulders on bed rolled along by traction (**transport**), collide and break up (**erosion**)

Smaller stones and pebbles bounced along river bed (**transport**), break down in size (**erosion**)

River bed

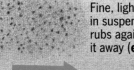

D

Most erosion occurs when a river is in flood. It can then carry huge amounts of material in suspension as well as being able to move the largest of boulders lying on its bed. Erosion can both deepen and widen a river valley (photo **D**). The valley deepens as a result of vertical erosion. This is more usual in mountainous areas nearer to the source of the river. Here the river forms a series of characteristic landforms which include a **V-shaped valley** with interlocking spurs (diagram **E**) as well as **waterfalls** and rapids (diagram **F**).

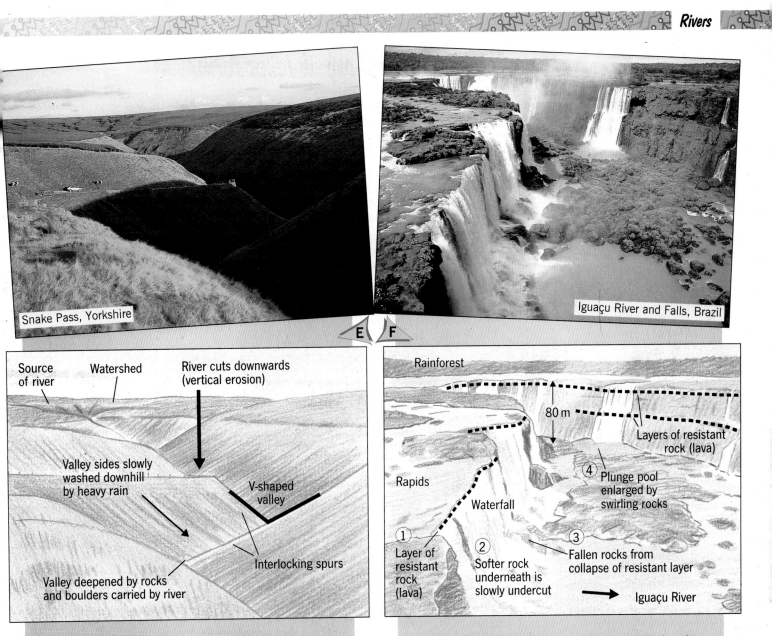

Snake Pass, Yorkshire

Iguaçu River and Falls, Brazil

Left diagram labels:
Source of river — Watershed — River cuts downwards (vertical erosion)

Valley sides slowly washed downhill by heavy rain

V-shaped valley

Interlocking spurs

Valley deepened by rocks and boulders carried by river

Right diagram labels:
Rainforest

80 m

Layers of resistant rock (lava)

Rapids

Waterfall

④ Plunge pool enlarged by swirling rocks

① Layer of resistant rock (lava)

② Softer rock underneath is slowly undercut

③ Fallen rocks from collapse of resistant layer

→ Iguaçu River

A river, especially when in flood, transports material along its bed. The material cuts downwards (vertical erosion) relatively quickly, deepening the bed of the river. After periods of heavy rain, soil on the valley sides slowly moves downhill under gravity. The valley forms a V-shape as it is deepened faster than it is widened.

The hard resistant surface rock is left unsupported as the underlying softer rock is eroded more quickly by the river. In time the resistant rock will collapse. This material will be swirled around by the river, widening and deepening the plunge pool at the foot of the waterfall. Over a period of time, as more rock collapses, the waterfall will slowly retreat leaving a steep-sided gorge.

Activities

1 Describe four processes by which a river might:
   a) erode its banks and bed
   b) transport material downstream.

2 a) Describe, with the help of neat and carefully labelled diagrams, how a river might form:
      i) a waterfall   ii) a V-shaped valley.
   b) For each answer, explain which processes of erosion and which processes of transportation affect its formation.

Summary

There are several processes by which rivers can erode the land and transport material. Together, these processes can produce a group of distinctive landforms which include V-shaped valleys and waterfalls.

▷ How do meanders and oxbow lakes form? ◁

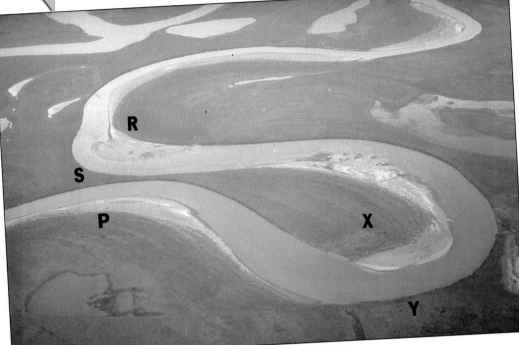

A Meander on North Slope River, Alaska

As rivers get nearer to their mouths they flow in increasingly wide, gentle-sided valleys. The channel increases in size to hold the extra water which the river has to receive from its tributaries. As the river gets bigger it can carry larger amounts of material. This material will be small in size, as larger rocks will have broken up on their way from the mountains. Much of the material will be carried in suspension and will erode the river banks by corrasion.

When rivers flow over flatter land, they develop large bends called **meanders** (photo **A**). As a river goes around a bend most of the water is pushed towards the outside causing increased erosion (diagram **C**). The river is now eroding sideways into its banks rather than downwards into its bed, a process called lateral erosion. On the inside of the bend, in contrast, there is much less water. The river will therefore be shallow and slow-flowing. It cannot carry as much material and so sand and shingle will be deposited. Diagram **B** is a cross-section showing the typical shape across a meander bend.

Due to erosion on the outside of a bend and deposition on the inside, the shape of a meander will change over a period of time (diagram **D**). Notice how erosion narrows the neck of the land within the meander. In time, and usually during a flood, the river will cut right through the neck. The river will take the new, shorter route (diagram **E**). The fastest current will now tend to be in the centre of the river, and so deposition is likely to occur in gentler water next to the banks. Eventually deposition will block off the old meander to leave an **oxbow lake** (photo **F**). The oxbow lake will slowly dry up, only refilling after heavy rain or during a flood.

Large rivers like the Mississippi and the Amazon have many oxbow lakes. Several new oxbow lakes were created following the Mississippi floods of mid-1993 (pages 18 and 19).

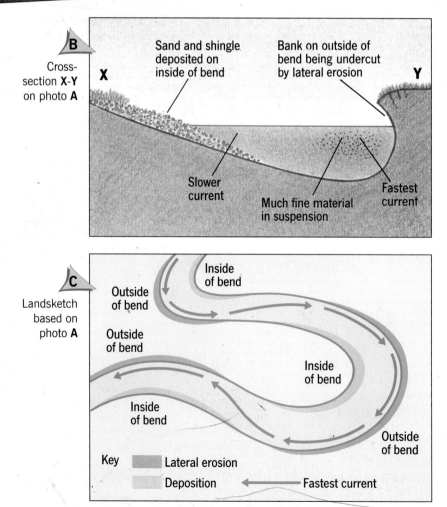

B Cross-section **X-Y** on photo **A**

Sand and shingle deposited on inside of bend
Bank on outside of bend being undercut by lateral erosion
Slower current
Much fine material in suspension
Fastest current

C Landsketch based on photo **A**

Inside of bend
Outside of bend
Outside of bend
Inside of bend
Inside of bend
Outside of bend

Key: Lateral erosion · Deposition · Fastest current

D Changing shape of a meander

Neck of land between loops gets narrower

Shape of meander in diagram **B**

New shape of meander

E Formation of an oxbow lake

Deposition

Oxbow or 'cut-off' lake

River cuts through narrow neck of land during flood

Fastest current is now in the middle of the river. Material is deposited in slower water near to river banks – including across the former meander

Key

| Land lost to the river (eroded) | ← Fastest current |
| Land gained from the river (deposited) | ------- Earlier course of river |

Activities

1 Using photo **A**, draw a cross-section from **P** to **R**. On your cross-section, label:
   a) the areas with the fastest current and the slowest current
   b) the places where erosion is taking place
   c) the places where deposition is taking place.

2 Describe, with the help of a diagram, what is likely to happen in the future at point **S** on photo **A**.

3 Diagram **G** is an incomplete cross-section of a meander. Copy and complete the diagram by using the following information:

Distance from left bank in metres	Depth of river in metres
0.5	1.0
0.75	2.0
1.0	3.0
2.0	3.25
3.0	3.0
4.0	2.5
5.0	2.0
6.0	1.0
7.0	0.5
8.0	0.0

4 If there is a small river or stream near to your school, take your own class measurements to produce a cross-section similar to the one in Activity **3**. But remember **to take care**. Serious accidents can occur in even small rivers and streams.

F Meanders and an oxbow lake, near Dalton in Yorkshire

G River meander

Surface of river

Depth of river (metres)

Distance from left bank (metres)

Summary

As most rivers approach the sea they begin to meander and, in some cases, to form oxbow lakes.

What is the relationship between precipitation and run-off?

The systems diagram (page 13) showed what happens once water has fallen to the Earth as precipitation. Rainwater, or melted snow, will either:

- be lost to the system through **evapotranspiration** (i.e. evaporation and transpiration)
- be held in storage in lakes, the soil or underground, or
- flow into a river to return, eventually, to the sea as run-off.

In other words, the amount of rainwater which will become the run-off of a river will be

Precipitation – (evapotranspiration + storage)

Under normal conditions, therefore, the run-off of a river will be less than precipitation. Precipitation and run-off figures for a year can be plotted graphically as in diagram **A**.

Precipitation and run-off are two variables. They are referred to as variables because the figures used to construct graph **A** are for one particular year. The figures will vary from one year to another. However, although the chances of the same figures being repeated in another year are highly unlikely, the relationship between the two variables is likely to remain similar, e.g. as the amount of precipitation increases so too does run-off.

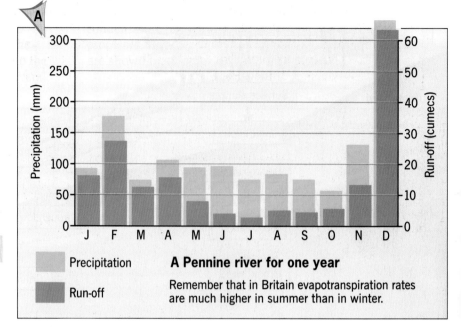

Precipitation
Run-off

A Pennine river for one year

Remember that in Britain evapotranspiration rates are much higher in summer than in winter.

Excess precipitation gives excess run-off which increases the risk of flooding.

The flood hydrograph

The amount of water in a river channel at a given time is called the **discharge**. Discharge is measured in cumecs (cubic metres of water per second). Following an increase in rainfall, there will also be an increase in the level and the discharge of the river. The relationship between precipitation and the level of a river is illustrated by the **flood** (or storm) **hydrograph** (diagram **B**).

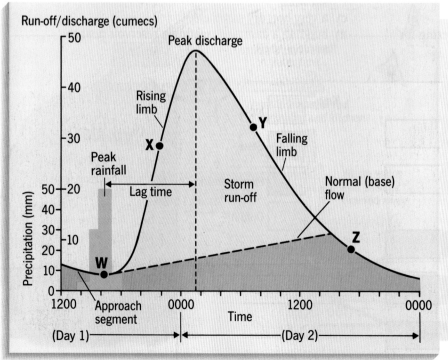

The **approach segment** shows the discharge of the river before it rains.

The **rising limb** results from a rapid increase in rainwater reaching the river.

Lag time is the difference between the time of the heaviest rainfall and the maximum level and/or discharge of the river.

The **falling limb** is when some rainwater is still reaching the river, but in decreasing amounts.

Points **W**, **X**, **Y** and **Z** are not usually shown on a flood hydrograph, but have been added here to help to explain its shape.

W – a very small amount of rain falls straight into the river channel.
X – water reaches the river rapidly by surface run-off.
Y – water reaches the river more slowly by throughflow.
Z – a limited amount of groundwater eventually reaches the river.

By showing the relationship between precipitation and run-off, the flood hydrograph indicates whether a particular river has a high or low flood risk. It therefore provides essential information for any river management scheme. The shorter the lag time and the steeper the rising limb, the greater is the flood risk. This is because much of the precipitation reaches the channel so quickly, mainly due to surface run-off, that the river has insufficient time to transport the excess water. In contrast, a river with a long lag time and a very gentle rising limb will have a very low flood risk. This is because rainwater reaches the channel slowly and over a longer period of time, allowing the river time to transport the excess water.

Activities

1 a) Using the information in table **C**, draw a graph to show the precipitation and run-off totals for a one-year period at a river recording site.

b) In which season are the figures at their highest for:
   i) precipitation
   ii) run-off?

c) Why is there a bigger difference between the precipitation and run-off totals in summer than in winter?

d) Suggest reasons why run-off was slightly higher than precipitation in March.

C ▷

	J	F	M	A	M	J	J	A	S	O	N	D
Precipitation (mm)	116	164	71	103	83	75	74	79	86	81	130	148
Run-off (mm)	103	143	79	84	47	17	22	26	41	64	106	125

2 Diagram **D** shows the hydrograph for a British river for three days.

a) i) How many hours did storm **1** last?
   ii) What was the time of peak rainfall in storm **1**?
   iii) How many hours was the lag time?

b) i) Why is there lag time between peak rainfall and peak discharge?
   ii) Why is the rising limb much steeper than the falling limb?
   iii) Give two reasons why discharge was higher after storm **2** than after storm **1**.

c) If the level of the river reached the top of its banks with a discharge of 70 cumecs, what must have happened after storm **2**?

D ▷

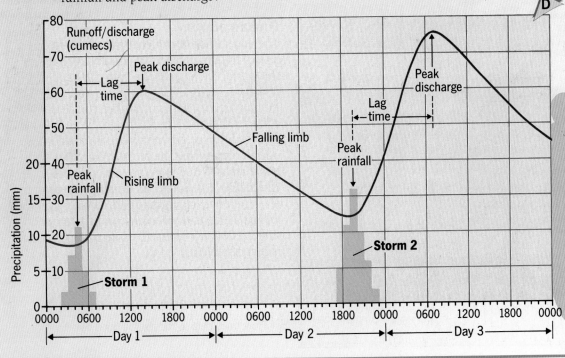

Summary

Precipitation and run-off are two variables. It is possible to identify a relationship between them showing that river run-off (discharge) depends upon the amount of precipitation. The flood hydrograph illustrates discharge and indicates the level of flood risk.

➤ *Why do some rivers flood?* ◀

Not every river has a high flood risk. However, those that do may flood for a combination of reasons. Often the four most important reasons are the:

- type and amount of precipitation
- type of soil and underlying rock
- land use of the river basin
- human activity.

Type and amount of precipitation

The most frequent cause of flooding is heavy rainfall which lasts over a period of several days. The ground will become saturated and infiltration will be replaced by surface run-off. The most severe cause of flooding usually

follows short, but very intense, thunderstorms. In Britain these storms are more likely to occur after a hot, dry spell in summer. The ground becomes too hard for the rain to infiltrate, and the surface run-off causes river levels to rise rapidly causing a **flash flood**.

Heavy snowfalls over several days mean that water is held in storage (photo **A**). When temperatures rise, there will be a release of water. The flood risk is greater if there is a large rise in temperature, if the rise is accompanied by a period of heavy rain, or if the ground remains frozen preventing infiltration.

Type of soil and underlying rock

Rocks that allow water to pass through them, like chalk, limestone and sandstone, are said to be **permeable**. Rocks that do not let water pass through them, such as granite, are **impermeable**. It is the same with soil. Sandy soils are permeable and allow water to infiltrate, whereas clay soils are impermeable. Surface run-off, and the flood risk, is much greater in river basins where the soil and underlying rock is impermeable.

Land use

River basins that have little vegetation cover have a much higher flood risk than forested river basins. This is because trees intercept rainfall, delaying the time and reducing the amount of water reaching the river (diagram **B**).

Human activity

There is sufficient evidence to prove that the risk of flooding is increasing in many parts of the world. The increase in both the frequency and the severity of flooding is usually linked to human activity, especially when this activity changes the land use of a basin through either deforestation or urban growth. Bangladesh is one country where the already high flood risk has increased due to deforestation in the Himalayas. Elsewhere, as urban areas grow in size, impermeable tarmac and concrete surfaces replace fields and woodland. Infiltration and throughflow are reduced, while surface run-off is increased (diagram **C**).

A Water held in storage: winter in the Yorkshire Dales

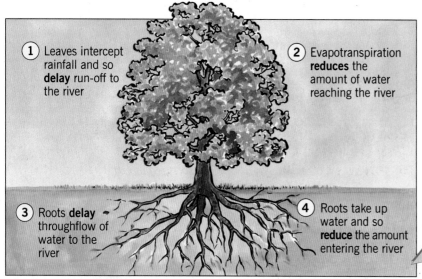

① Leaves intercept rainfall and so **delay** run-off to the river

② Evapotranspiration **reduces** the amount of water reaching the river

③ Roots **delay** throughflow of water to the river

④ Roots take up water and so **reduce** the amount entering the river

B How trees help to reduce the flood risk

Drains and gutters are constructed to remove surface water. This might decrease the time taken by rainwater to reach the river, but it increases the risk of a flash flood. Small streams are forced to travel along culverts (photo **D**) or underground pipes. Drains and underground pipes may not be large enough to cope with rainwater falling during thunderstorms.

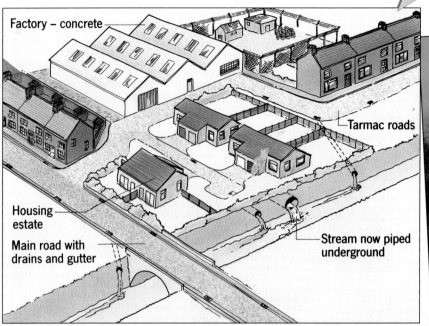

Factory – concrete

Tarmac roads

Housing estate

Main road with drains and gutter

Stream now piped underground

C

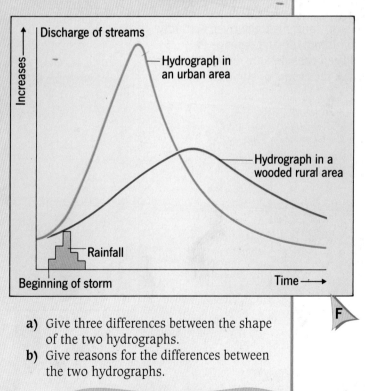

D

Activities

1 Explain why there is a high flood risk:
   a) after a long period of heavy rainfall
   b) after a summer thunderstorm
   c) when a heavy snowfall follows a few days when temperatures remained below freezing
   d) in an area with an impermeable underlying rock
   e) in a river basin that has just been deforested.

2 Copy and complete diagram **E** to show how the river basin system (diagram **C**, page 13) is changed by urban growth.

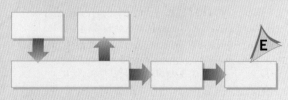

E

3 Diagram **F** shows flood hydrographs following a rainstorm for a stream in a wooded rural area and a stream in a nearby urban area.

Discharge of streams

Increases

Hydrograph in an urban area

Hydrograph in a wooded rural area

Rainfall

Beginning of storm

Time →

F

a) Give three differences between the shape of the two hydrographs.
b) Give reasons for the differences between the two hydrographs.

Summary

The risk of a river flooding depends upon several factors including the type and amount of precipitation, soil, underlying rock, and land use. Recently the risk has increased due to human activities which have led to deforestation, and urban growth.

17

What were the causes and effects of the Mississippi flood?

The Mississippi River is 3800 km in length and flows through ten states. It receives over 100 major tributaries, including the Missouri which joins it at St Louis (map **A**). Its drainage basin covers one-third of the USA and a small part of Canada (map **E**, page 5).

Frequent flooding by the Mississippi has created a wide flood plain. The flood plain is 200 km at its widest point, and consists of fertile silt deposited by the river at times of flood. Even before the area was settled by Europeans, the river flowed above the level of its flood plain and between natural levées (page 10). Nineteenth-century Americans considered the Mississippi to be 'untameable', and a major flood in 1927 caused 217 deaths. Since then over 300 dams and storage reservoirs have been built, and natural levées have been heightened and strengthened to protect major urban areas. The levée at St Louis is 18 km long and 16 metres high. Flooding continued throughout the 1950s and 1960s, but the last big flood was in 1973. The Americans believed that, due to large investments of money and modern technology, they had at least 'controlled' the river. Certainly, the danger to human life and damage to property had been considerably reduced. . . but that was before the events of summer 1993.

A

The Mississippi floods, 1993

N

Mississippi R.

Canada
USA

Lake Superior

Lake Michigan

Minneapolis • St Paul

Missouri R.

Raccoon R.

• Omaha • Des Moines

Chicago •

Flooded area

Kansas City

• St Louis

Ohio R.

British Isles to same scale

Memphis •

Tennessee R.

Arkansas R.

Mississippi R.

0   200 km

New Orleans

Gulf of Mexico

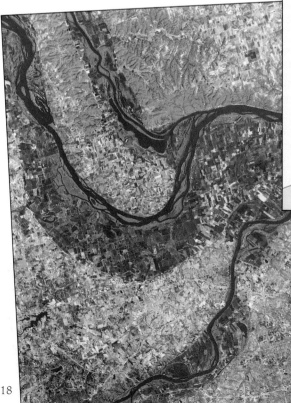

B

The Mississippi and Missouri Rivers as they approach their confluence above St Louis. The bluish-purple colour shows the flooded area.

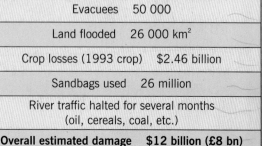

Deaths	43
Evacuees	50 000
Land flooded	26 000 km²
Crop losses (1993 crop)	$2.46 billion
Sandbags used	26 million
River traffic halted for several months (oil, cereals, coal, etc.)	
Overall estimated damage	**$12 billion (£8 bn)**

C

The 1993 flood at St Louis

- Height of levée (15.8 m)
- 1993 flood peak (15.05 m)
- Previous highest flood level (12.3 m)
- Flood level (9 m)
- Usual river level (4 m)
- Height of St Louis

D Mississippi river floods, 1993

Heavy rain in April 1993 saturated the upper Mississippi basin. Thunderstorms throughout June caused rapid surface run-off and flash floods (page 16). During July the thunderstorms increased in severity with one giving 180 mm of rain in a few hours. By mid-July the level of the Mississippi had reached an all-time high (diagram **C**). Levées surrounding towns were put under tremendous pressure from the weight of water in the river, and in many places they collapsed (photo **B**). Away from towns the river spread across its flood plain up to a width of 25 km (photo **D**). An area larger than the British Isles was affected by flooding (map **A**). Only one road bridge, and no rail bridge, remained open for 400 km north of St Louis. River traffic on one of the world's busiest highways had long since been brought to a stop. The Mississippi proved it had not been

tamed, as it claimed lives and destroyed property (map **A**). Many Americans felt that the effects of the flood had been made worse unintentionally, because people had interfered with nature in trying to manage and control the river.

The effects of the flood did not end when the river levels began to fall. It took several months for the water to drain off the land. Although the land was covered in fertile silt, the ground was too wet for planting crops. The contents of houses and factories, even if not the buildings themselves, were ruined. Cleaning-up operations took months. Where sewage had been washed into waterways, there was a threat of disease. Stagnant water attracted mosquitos and rats. Insurance claims were high and numerous.

Activities

1 a) Why is the Mississippi a high flood risk river?
   b) What caused the flood of 1993?
   c) What were the immediate effects of the flood?
   d) What might be some of the long-term effects of the flood?

2 How had human activity unintentionally increased the flood risk?

Summary

When rivers flood they can put lives in danger, damage property and disrupt people's normal way of life. Sometimes attempts to reduce the flood risk can unintentionally make the effects of flooding worse.

How do waves wear away the land?

Although waves may sometimes result from submarine Earth movements (page 59), they are usually formed by the wind blowing over the sea. The size of a wave depends upon the:

- strength of the wind
- length of time that the wind blows
- distance of sea that the wind has to cross.

As a wave approaches shallow water near to the coast, its base is slowed down by friction against the sea-bed. The top of the wave will therefore move faster, increase in height and will eventually break ('tumble over') onto the beach.

Coastal erosion

There are four main processes by which the sea can erode the land. These are similar to those of a river (page 6).

- **Hydraulic pressure** is the sheer force of the waves, especially when they trap and compress air in cracks and holes in a cliff.
- **Corrasion** results from large waves hurling beach material against the cliff.
- **Attrition** is when waves cause rocks and pebbles on the beach to bump into each other and to break down in size.
- **Corrosion** is when certain types of cliff are slowly dissolved by acids in the sea-water.

There are three main groups of landforms which result from erosion by the sea.

Headlands and bays These form along coasts which have alternating resistant (harder) and less resistant (softer) rock. Where there is resistant rock the coast will be worn away less quickly leaving a **headland** which sticks out into the sea. Where there is softer rock, erosion will be more rapid and a **bay** will form (diagram **A** and page 48). As the headland becomes more exposed to the full force of the wind and waves, it will become more vulnerable to erosion than the sheltered bay.

A

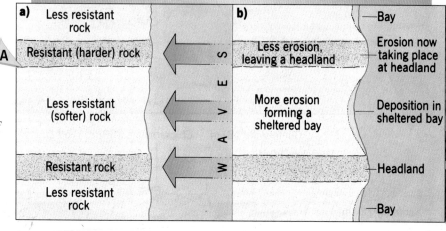

a)

| Less resistant rock |
| Resistant (harder) rock |
| Less resistant (softer) rock |
| Resistant rock |
| Less resistant rock |

W A V E S

b)

Less erosion, leaving a headland — Bay

Erosion now taking place at headland

More erosion forming a sheltered bay — Deposition in sheltered bay

Headland

Bay

Cliffs and wave-cut platforms Erosion is greatest when large waves actually break against the foot of a cliff. The foot of the cliff is undercut to form a **wave-cut notch** (diagram **B**). As the notch gets larger, the cliff above it will become increasingly unsupported and in time will collapse. As this process is repeated the cliff will slowly retreat and, usually, increase in height. The gently sloping land left at the foot of the retreating cliff is called a **wave-cut platform** (diagram **B**).

B

③ Cliff increases in height

② Cliff retreats

① Original position of cliff

High water mark

Wave-cut notch

Low water mark

Wave-cut platform

b) Wave-cut platform

a) Wave-cut notch

Caves, arches and stacks Although cliffs, especially where they form headlands, consist of resistant rock they are still likely to contain areas of weakness. Areas of weakness will be the first to be worn away by the sea. Diagram **C** shows a typical sequence in which a weakness is enlarged to form a **cave** and, later, an **arch** where the sea cuts right through the headland. The arch is widened by the sea undercutting at its base. As the rock above the arch becomes unsupported it collapses to form a **stack**. Further undercutting causes the stack to collapse leaving only a stump.

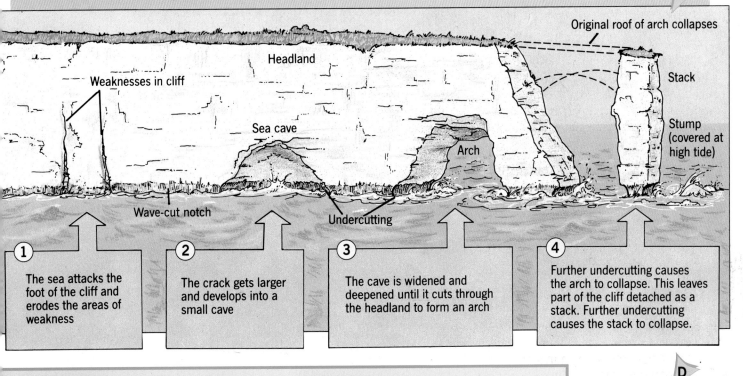

C

Original roof of arch collapses

Headland

Weaknesses in cliff

Stack

Sea cave

Arch

Stump (covered at high tide)

Wave-cut notch

Undercutting

1 The sea attacks the foot of the cliff and erodes the areas of weakness

2 The crack gets larger and develops into a small cave

3 The cave is widened and deepened until it cuts through the headland to form an arch

4 Further undercutting causes the arch to collapse. This leaves part of the cliff detached as a stack. Further undercutting causes the stack to collapse.

Activities

1 Give three reasons why, on diagram **D**, the waves at **X** are likely to be higher and more powerful than the waves at **Y**.

2 Describe briefly four processes by which the sea can erode the land.

3 Photo **E** shows several coastal features.
   a) Make a landsketch of the photo and add the following labels:
      • *corrasion by waves*
      • *wave-cut notch*
      • *wave-cut platform*
      • *cave* • *arch* • *stacks*.
   b) Use broken lines to show the position of two collapsed arches.

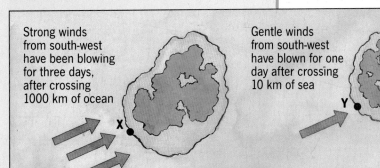

D

Strong winds from south-west have been blowing for three days, after crossing 1000 km of ocean

X

Gentle winds from south-west have blown for one day after crossing 10 km of sea

Y

E

Old Harry Rocks, Dorset

Summary

Waves are caused when the wind blows over the surface of the sea. There are four processes by which the sea can erode the land to produce such landforms as headlands, bays, cliffs, wave-cut platforms and stacks.

23

How does the sea transport material?

Material can be moved both along and up and down a beach.

Transportation along a beach Waves rarely approach a beach at right-angles. They usually approach at an angle that depends upon the direction of the wind (diagram **A**). The water that rushes up a beach after a wave breaks is called the swash. The swash, which picks up sand and shingle, travels up the beach in the same direction as the breaking wave. When this water returns down the beach to the sea it is called backwash. Due to gravity the backwash, and any material it is carrying, tends to be straight down the beach (diagram **A**). The result is that material is transported along the beach in a zig-zag movement. This movement of beach material is called **longshore drift**. Longshore drift is usually in one direction only, that of the prevailing wind. For example, the prevailing wind in Britain is from the south-west and so material is moved from west to east along the south coast of England.

A

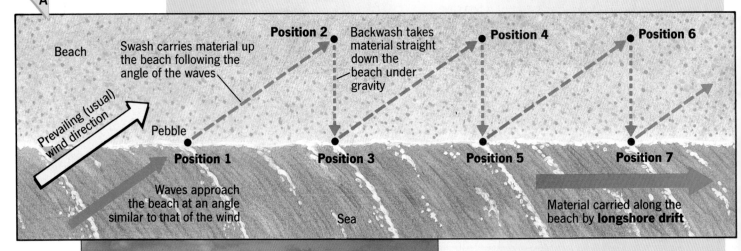

Beach

Swash carries material up the beach following the angle of the waves

Prevailing (usual) wind direction

Pebble

Position 2

Backwash takes material straight down the beach under gravity

Position 4

Position 6

Position 1

Waves approach the beach at an angle similar to that of the wind

Position 3

Sea

Position 5

Position 7

Material carried along the beach by **longshore drift**

Longshore drift can sometimes affect human activities. In response, people sometimes erect wooden breakwater fences down the beach (photos **B a)** and **b)**). The fences, called groynes, reduce the force of the waves and cause sand to pile up on their windward side (the side facing the prevailing wind). This is an advantage to people living in a seaside resort who do not wish to lose their sand and to sailors in a small port who do not want their harbour to become blocked.

B

a) Longshore drift, Dungeness in Kent

b) Groynes at a British coastal resort

Transportation up and down a beach
Under normal conditions waves will tend to move material up a beach. Photo **C** shows how shingle has been piled up at the foot of a cliff. The shingle will, in this case, protect the cliff from erosion. However, under storm conditions, larger waves often move material back down the beach.

How can human activities affect the rate of landform development?

We have already seen that the building of groynes can slow down the transport of material along the beach. Around many parts of our coastline sea walls have been constructed to try to reduce the force of the waves and to protect cliffs from erosion. Sometimes, however, human activity can unintentionally speed up the rate at which cliffs are eroded. During one year at the end of the last century, 660 000 tonnes of shingle were removed from the beach at Hallsands in Devon. It was used for the construction of the naval dockyard at Plymouth. The speed at which the shingle was removed was far greater than the rate at which nature could replace it. The cliff was exposed to erosion and within a century it had retreated by almost 10 metres. Buildings in Hallsands became threatened as the cliff retreated and the village has now been left virtually abandoned and in ruins (photo **D**).

C Shingle at the foot of cliffs at Weybourne, Norfolk

D Deserted village of Hallsands, Devon

Activity

- What name is given to the process by which material is moved along a stretch of coastline?
- How can waves transport sand from point **A** to point **X** on diagram **E**?
- Why might people in each of a) place **R** and b) place **S** want to reduce the movement of material along the beach?
- How might they stop material from point **A** moving to point **X**?

- How might waves move material from point **A** to point **Y**?
- A building firm applied to the local council for permission to remove shingle from point **Y**. Why do you think that their application was turned down?

E

Small port

Seaside resort

S

Harbour

R

X

Y

A

Summary The movement of material along a beach is called longshore drift. Human activities can affect the rate at which coastal landforms develop.

How do landforms result from deposition by the sea?

Deposition occurs in sheltered areas where the build-up of sand and shingle is greater than its removal. The most widespread coastal deposition feature is the beach. Although rocky beaches are formed by erosion (wave-cut platforms, page 22), sand and shingle beaches result from deposition. Diagram **A** shows the differences in steepness between sand and shingle beaches, and how material of different sizes is distributed on those beaches.

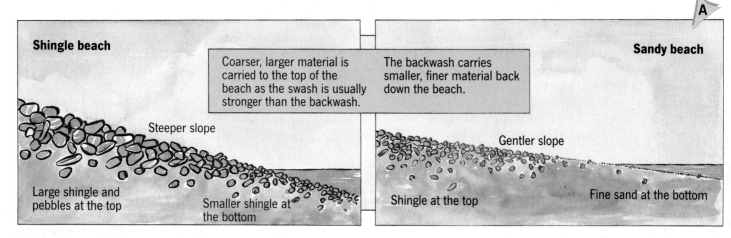

Shingle beach

Coarser, larger material is carried to the top of the beach as the swash is usually stronger than the backwash.

The backwash carries smaller, finer material back down the beach.

Sandy beach

Steeper slope

Large shingle and pebbles at the top

Smaller shingle at the bottom

Gentler slope

Shingle at the top

Fine sand at the bottom

Spits

A **spit** is an area of sand or shingle which either extends at a gentle angle out to sea or which grows across a river estuary (diagrams **B** and **C**). Many spits are characterised by a hooked, or curved, end. Spits only develop in places where:

- longshore drift moves large amounts of material along the beach
- there is a sudden change in the direction of the coastline
- the sea is relatively shallow and becomes progressively more sheltered.

Diagram **B** shows how a typical spit forms. The line **X–Y** marks the position of the original coastline. The prevailing wind, in this example, is from the south-west and so material is carried eastwards by longshore drift (**A**). Where the coastline changes direction (**B**), sand and shingle are deposited in water which is sheltered by the headland. This material builds upwards and outwards (**C**) forming a spit. Occasionally strong winds blow from a different direction, in this case the south-east. As waves will now also approach the land from the south-east, then some material will be pushed inland causing the end of the spit to curve (**D**). When the wind returns to its usual direction the spit will continue to grow eastwards (**E**), developing further hooked ends during times of changed wind direction (**F**). The spit cannot grow across the estuary (**G**) due to the speed of the river carrying material out to sea. Spits become permanent when the prevailing wind picks up sand from the beach and blows it inland to form sand dunes. Salt marsh (**H**) develops in the sheltered water behind the spit.

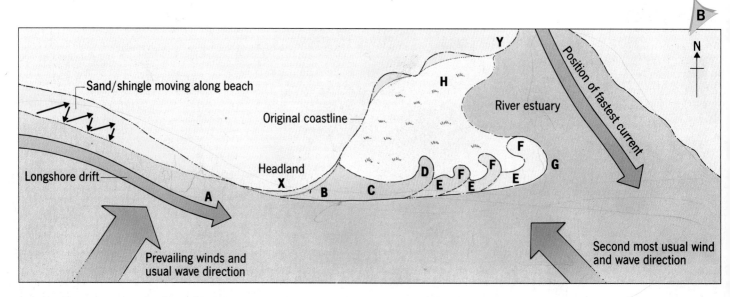

Sand/shingle moving along beach

Original coastline

Headland

Longshore drift

River estuary

Position of fastest current

Prevailing winds and usual wave direction

Second most usual wind and wave direction

C Dawlish Warren, Devon

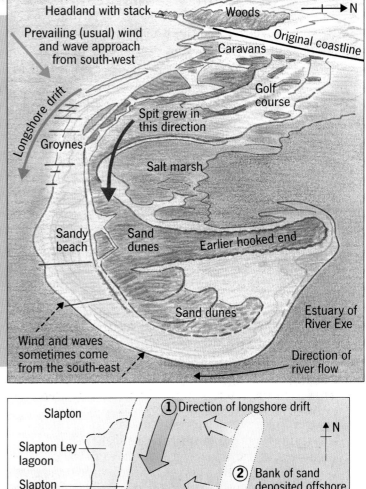

Headland with stack
Woods
Prevailing (usual) wind and wave approach from south-west
Original coastline
Caravans
Longshore drift
Spit grew in this direction
Golf course
Groynes
Salt marsh
Sandy beach
Sand dunes
Earlier hooked end
Wind and waves sometimes come from the south-east
Sand dunes
Estuary of River Exe
Direction of river flow
N

Bars

A **bar** is a barrier of sand stretching across a sheltered bay. It is only able to extend across the bay due to the absence of any large river (diagram **D**). Bars may form in several ways. One way is when a spit is able to grow right across a bay. A second is when a sand bank develops some distance off the shore, but parallel to it. Waves slowly move the sand bank towards the coast until it joins with the mainland. In both cases a lagoon is usually found to the landward side of the bar.

D

Slapton
Slapton Ley lagoon
Slapton Sands
Spit eventually extends across a small bay
① Direction of longshore drift
N
② Bank of sand deposited offshore slowly migrates towards the land
0   1 km

Activities

1 How does the appearance of a sandy beach differ from that of a shingle beach?

2 The following sketches show several stages in the formation of a spit. Unfortunately they are not in the correct order.
   a) Redraw the sketches putting the stages into the correct order.
   b) Describe how each stage developed.

E

Summary

Sand and shingle are deposited where the sea is calm and gentle. Beaches, spits and bars are examples of landforms which result from deposition.

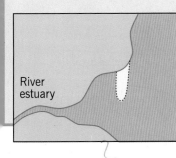

River estuary

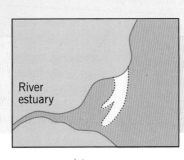

River estuary

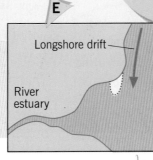

Longshore drift

River estuary

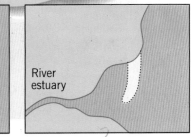

River estuary

Coastal flooding in Britain

The worst coastal flood in recent years in Britain occurred during the night of 31 January/1 February 1953. The worst affected area was between the estuaries of the Humber and the Thames.

Causes

Most of the area between the Humber and the Thames is low-lying. Indeed, some parts surrounding The Wash are actually below sea-level. These areas were protected by small sea walls and embankments, many of which were in a state of disrepair due to a lack of attention during and after the Second World War. Although people realised that there was a high flood risk, they were totally unprepared for that night in 1953. Four main factors combined to cause a **storm** (or **tidal**) **surge**. A storm surge is when the level of the sea rises rapidly to a height well above that which was predicted.

1 An area of low atmospheric pressure, called a depression, moved southwards into the North Sea. Air rises in a depression. As the air rose it exerted less pressure, or weight, upon the sea. The reduction in pressure was enough to allow the surface of the sea to rise by half a metre.

2 The severe northerly gale created huge 6-metre high waves. These waves 'pushed' sea-water southwards down the North Sea to where it gets shallower and narrower, as shown on map **A**. As the extra water 'surged' southwards, it was unable to escape fast enough through the Straits of Dover. The result was a further 2-metre rise in sea-level, especially in river estuaries.

3 It was a time of spring tides. These occur every month and are when the tides reach their highest level.

4 Rivers flowing into the North Sea were in flood but could not discharge their water due to the high sea-levels.

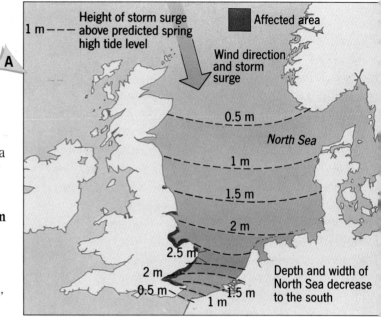

A

Consequences

The flood caused the deaths of 264 people and damage to 25 000 homes (map **B** and photos **C** and **D**). Sea-water covered over 1000 m² of land in Lincolnshire, East Anglia and the Thames Estuary. Thousands of farm animals were drowned. The high death rate among humans and animals was partly due to the flood being unexpected and no advance warnings being given. The greatest loss of human life was in places where people were asleep in bungalows. Even when the flood subsided, sea water was still able to penetrate gaps in sea defences, and farmland remained contaminated by salt water. The disaster was even worse across the North Sea where, in the Netherlands, more than 1800 people died.

B

TIMETABLE		
Saturday 31 January 1953:		
a.m.	Aberdeen	Gales with gusts of 130 km/h (80 mph)
15.30	River Tees	Water overflows banks
17.00	Lincolnshire	Flooding along coast, 16 die and 1600 evacuated at Mablethorpe. 20 die as Skegness is flooded.
19.15	Norfolk	Train forced back to Hunstanton as waves break through sand dunes, engulfing village and killing 65
22.18	Southend	Tanker *Kosmos V* runs aground
Midnight	Isle of Sheppey	Much of island, including naval dockyard, flooded
Sunday 1 February:		
00.30	Harwich	1200 homes flooded, eight die
00.30	Southend	600 homes engulfed, two killed
00.40	Tilbury	Thames overflows, killing one and making 6102 homeless
01.10	Canvey Island	11 000 homeless, 58 dead
01.55	Canning Town	Sea breaks in, making 150 homeless, killing one

Low pressure

Northern gales and surge tides

Aberdeen

River Tees

Mablethorpe
Skegness
Hunstanton
Southend
London
Canning Town

Harwich

Canvey Island

Isle of Sheppey

Tilbury

France

C

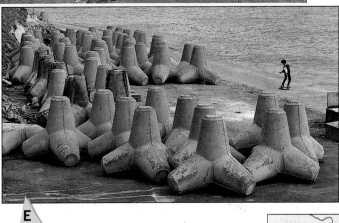

D

Responses

- The first response was to build stronger sea defences and higher embankments. At first concrete was used to 'bounce' storm waves back out to sea. However, it was realised that the power of storm waves limited the life span of a concrete defence to under 30 years. Modern sea defences use either cages filled with stones, or sloping wooden fences (photo **E**). The idea is to reduce the power of the waves by allowing some of the water to pass through the structures.
- Sand and shingle is now dumped offshore to reduce the power and the height of the waves.
- A storm tide early warning system gives at least 12 hours' notice of extra high tides.
- The building of the Thames Barrier to reduce the flood risk in London (photo **F**).

F   The Thames Barrier at Woolwich

E

G

Activity

Those parts of India and Bangladesh which border the Bay of Bengal have a high risk of coastal flooding resulting from storm surges (map **G**).

- What is a storm surge?
- Give three reasons why the Bay of Bengal experiences storm surges.
- What were the consequences of the storm surge that affected the east coast of England in 1953?
- What has been done to try to reduce the effect of future storm surges in eastern England?
- Why do you think similar precautions have not been taken in those areas around the Bay of Bengal?

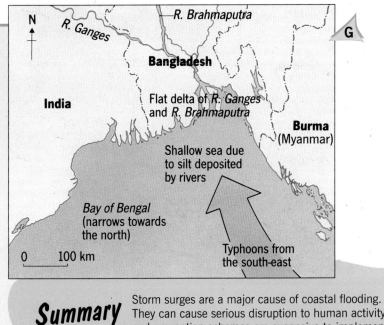

N

R. Brahmaputra

R. Ganges

Bangladesh

India

Flat delta of *R. Ganges* and *R. Brahmaputra*

Burma (Myanmar)

Shallow sea due to silt deposited by rivers

Bay of Bengal (narrows towards the north)

0   100 km

Typhoons from the south-east

Summary   Storm surges are a major cause of coastal flooding. They can cause serious disruption to human activity and prevention schemes are expensive to implement.

How do changes in sea-level affect landforms?

Sea-level has rarely stayed constant for a lengthy period of time. It has risen and fallen, usually due to Earth movements or changes in climate. Changes in sea-level can either create new landforms or submerge existing ones.

At the beginning of the Ice Age large amounts of water were held in storage as ice and snow (page 12). With no water

being returned to the oceans, sea-level fell. At the end of the Ice Age, the melting of glaciers led to a release of water and a rise in sea-level. Many coastal areas were drowned and new landforms, such as **fjords** and **rias**, were formed (diagram **A**).

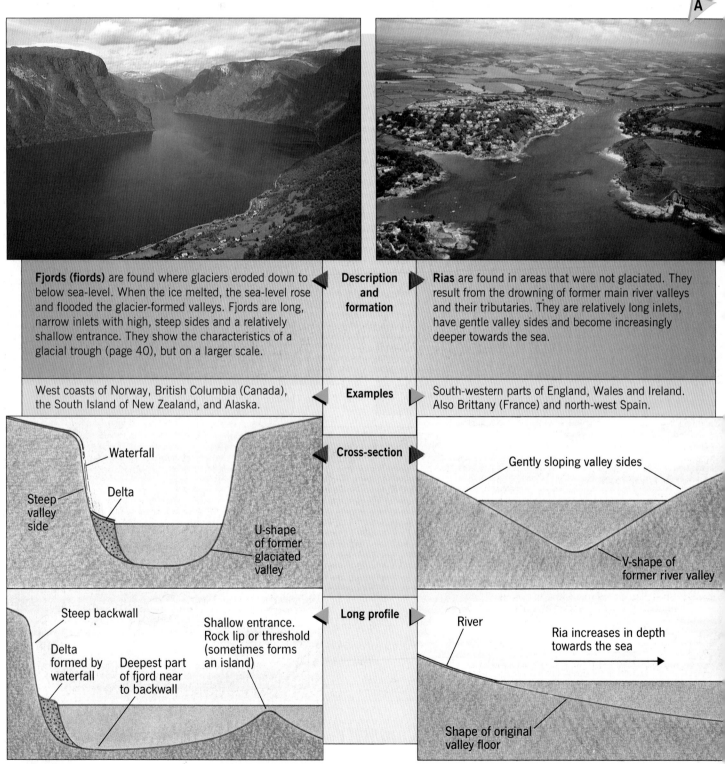

A

Fjords (fiords) are found where glaciers eroded down to below sea-level. When the ice melted, the sea-level rose and flooded the glacier-formed valleys. Fjords are long, narrow inlets with high, steep sides and a relatively shallow entrance. They show the characteristics of a glacial trough (page 40), but on a larger scale.	**Description and formation**	Rias are found in areas that were not glaciated. They result from the drowning of former main river valleys and their tributaries. They are relatively long inlets, have gentle valley sides and become increasingly deeper towards the sea.
West coasts of Norway, British Columbia (Canada), the South Island of New Zealand, and Alaska.	**Examples**	South-western parts of England, Wales and Ireland. Also Brittany (France) and north-west Spain.
	Cross-section	
	Long profile	

Cross-section (fjord):
Waterfall
Delta
Steep valley side
U-shape of former glaciated valley

Cross-section (ria):
Gently sloping valley sides
V-shape of former river valley

Long profile (fjord):
Steep backwall
Delta formed by waterfall
Deepest part of fjord near to backwall
Shallow entrance. Rock lip or threshold (sometimes forms an island)

Long profile (ria):
River
Ria increases in depth towards the sea
Shape of original valley floor

How might global warming affect coasts?

During this century, average world temperatures have risen by 0.5 °C. Many scientists predict that the Earth's temperature will continue to increase, perhaps by 1.5 °C by the year 2030. One consequence of this **global warming** will be a melting of some of the polar ice-cap. Melting ice will increase the flow of water into the sea, causing levels to rise by anything up to 3 metres. Although this rise in sea-level will be small in comparison with that at the end of the Ice Age, it will still flood many low-lying coastal areas. Map **B** shows the most vulnerable areas. Worst hit will be some Pacific islands, which will be totally submerged, and large river deltas. In Egypt (map **C**) a rise in sea-level of 0.5 metres would swamp the main ports of Alexandria and Port Said and ruin the fishing industry in the coastal lagoons. A rise of 1 metre would flood 30 per cent of Egypt's arable land and displace 8 million people (remember the 1953 coastal surge in eastern England was 2.5 metres).

Map **D** shows places in Britain that are vulnerable to a rise in sea-level. The compilers of this map assume that sea-levels will increase by 0.5 to 1.5 metres within the next century. The effect of such a rise would include a loss of beaches, an increase in coastal erosion, a loss of wetland and other wildlife habitats, and the drowning of cities and low-lying farmland. A United Nations-backed agency estimates the cost to Britain of combating rising sea-levels will be over £6.5 billion (bn) next century. Of this, £2.6 bn will be needed to protect coastal cities from inundation, £0.7 bn to safeguard harbours and ports, £2 bn to defend low-lying coastal land, and £1.2 bn to rescue beaches.

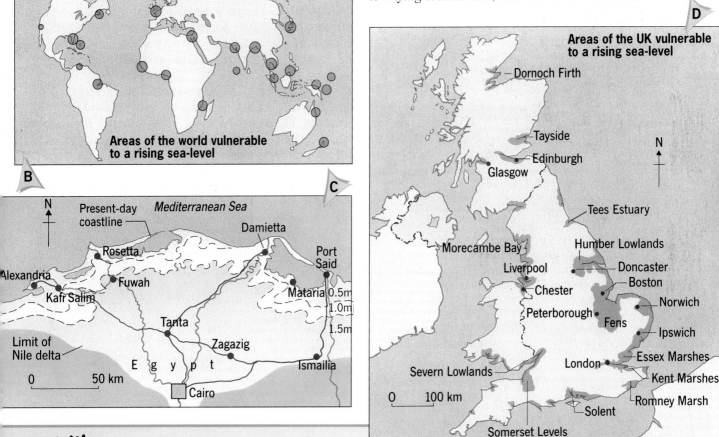

B Areas of the world vulnerable to a rising sea-level

C Mediterranean Sea — Present-day coastline, Damietta, Rosetta, Port Said, Alexandria, Fuwah, Mataria 0.5m, Kafr Salim, 1.0m, Tanta, 1.5m, Zagazig, Limit of Nile delta, E g y p t, Ismailia, 0 50 km, Cairo

D Areas of the UK vulnerable to a rising sea-level — Dornoch Firth, Tayside, Edinburgh, Glasgow, Tees Estuary, Morecambe Bay, Humber Lowlands, Liverpool, Doncaster, Boston, Chester, Norwich, Peterborough, Fens, Ipswich, Severn Lowlands, London, Essex Marshes, Kent Marshes, Romney Marsh, Solent, Somerset Levels, 0 100 km

Activities

1 a) Why did sea-levels rise after the Ice Age?
  b) Describe the main differences between fjords and rias under these headings:
  • Formation • Appearance
  • Cross-section shape • Long profile.

2 Global warming is likely to cause a rise in the world's sea-level.
  a) Which parts of the world are at greatest risk from flooding by the sea?
  b) What effect will a rise in sea-level have upon Egypt?

c) Many parts of Britain are also at risk from a rise in sea-level.
  i) Which parts of Britain have the highest risk from coastal flooding?
  ii) How will a rise in sea-level affect human activities in these parts of Britain?
  iii) Why might Britain have to spend £6.5 billion to combat a rise in sea-level?

Summary

Changes in sea-level affect coasts. The large rise in sea-level after the Ice Age created new landforms. A small rise due to global warming is expected to drown many low-lying areas.

3 Water pollution

▷ What causes water pollution? ◁

In England and Wales in 1994, 89 per cent of rivers and canals were of good or fair water quality (graph **A**). However, since 1980 there had been a slight decline in water quality. In 1994 there were 30 740 reported pollution incidents, more than in previous years. This figure did not include the increasing occurrences of algal blooms, which are excessive growths of algae caused by nitrate pollution (photo **D**, page 127). Graph **B** shows the major types of reported pollution incidents.

Sewage disposal Most sewage is sent to treatment works where waste products are removed, leaving sewage sludge (page 34). The resultant effluent, which should be 95 per cent waste water, is discharged into rivers. However, there is still about one-quarter of the population not served by sewage treatment works. It is from this source that untreated sewage may reach rivers.

Agricultural run-off Farm waste and silage effluent are normally spread on farmland, but accidents, careless use, and periods of heavy rain can lead to them reaching a river and causing serious pollution. Undiluted farm slurry (animal waste) is 100 times more polluting than raw sewage, and silage effluent (from grass fermenting in storage) is 200 times more polluting. Bacteria in rivers use up large amounts of oxygen to break down the slurry and silage. This leaves the river short of oxygen, causing damage to fish and other water life. Fertiliser, including nitrate, is added to crops to encourage growth. If the nitrate reaches a river, it will cause excessive plant growth (including algal blooms) which also results in deoxygenation.

Industrial discharge Some industrial waste is discharged directly into the river. Some of this waste, especially that containing chemicals, can be extremely harmful to river life, can discolour the water, and may give off an odious smell.

Power stations Many power stations extract water for cooling purposes before returning it, at a much higher temperature, to the river (page 132). Although the warm water does not actually pollute the river, it can harm river life as it contains less oxygen.

Landfill sites Pollutants from waste landfill sites can leach slowly into rivers. Diagram **C** shows how these various types of pollution can reach the river and, eventually, the sea.

A Water quality of rivers and canals in England and Wales, 1994

Anglian
Northumbria & Yorks
North West
Severn Trent
Southern
South West
Thames
Welsh

0   20   40   60   80   100%

Source: HMSO, *Regional Trends*, 1996

Good quality (class 1)
High quality – suitable for drinking water. High-quality fishing. High recreation value.

Fair quality (class 2)
Suitable for drinking water after extensive treatment. Good fishing. Moderate recreation value.

Poor quality (class 3)
Polluted. Fish either absent or only sporadically present. Unsuitable for drinking purposes. Low-grade industrial abstract. Low recreation value.

Bad quality (class 4)
Heavily polluted. Likely to cause health and environmental problems.

B Water pollution: Class 1 incidents in England and Wales, 1995

Source: NRA, 1996

Others 21%
Sewage 24%
Transport 8%
Industry 9%
Agriculture 16%
Oil 22%

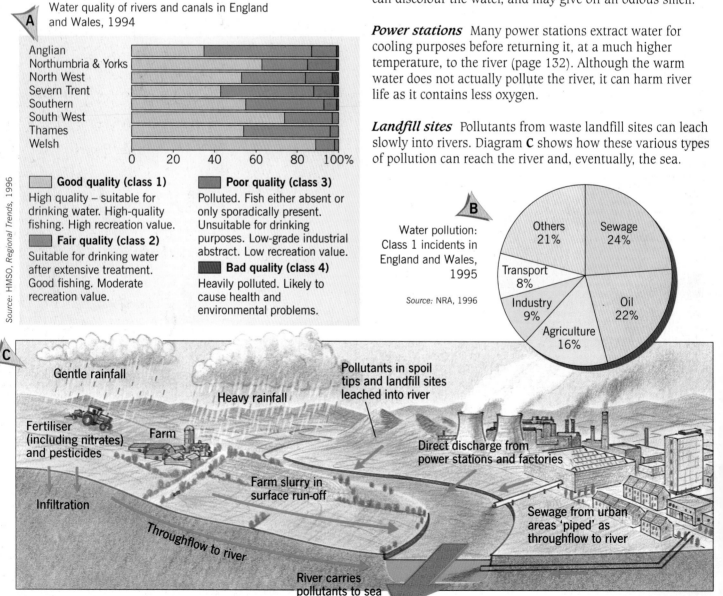

C

Gentle rainfall

Heavy rainfall

Pollutants in spoil tips and landfill sites leached into river

Fertiliser (including nitrates) and pesticides

Farm

Direct discharge from power stations and factories

Infiltration

Farm slurry in surface run-off

Throughflow to river

Sewage from urban areas 'piped' as throughflow to river

River carries pollutants to sea

The Ganges, in India, is a sacred river to the Hindus. It is also severely polluted, as described in **D**.

The Ganges is one of the Earth's longest and most polluted rivers. It descends from the Himalayas some 2500 km across India before it fans into the Bay of Bengal.

It poses a unique dilemma for environmentalists. Every year, Hindus dump more than 45 000 bodies in the Ganges, first inserting a red-hot coal into the mouth of each corpse before casting it adrift. No sane ecologist would ever dare to prevent this. Hindus believe that the Ganges can free the dying from the cycle of rebirth, so in many river cities, such as Varanasi, Calcutta and Allahabad, ashes from the cremation pyres are sprinkled into the river. Dead babies, lepers, suicides, people killed by snakebites and sages are also given a river burial. Sometimes, too, in Varanasi the body-burners scrimp on wood for the pyre and simply toss the half-charred remains into the river, just upstream from where thousands of Hindus bathe every day.

The main pollutants, however, are not dead bodies but the waste spewed into the Ganges from hundreds of factories, tanneries, petro-chemical plants, paper mills and sugar refineries along its banks. The Ganges provides water for more than 250 million people living in the flat, hot Gangetic plains. It irrigates their crops and quenches their spiritual thirst. At its source, in the Himalayan glaciers above Gangotri, it is a fast, shining-white stream. By the time it reaches Patna, the Ganges has widened to 10 km and begins to divide itself into a delta before reaching the ocean. At one time there were freshwater dolphins, giant 6-metre crocodiles, turtles and more than 265 species of fish living in the Ganges. Six years ago environmentalists calculated that 1000 million litres of waste water a day were pouring into the Ganges. If left unchecked, the sacred river would die.

Adapted from The Independent on Sunday *, 9 August 1992*

Activities

1 a) Which region in England and Wales has the highest percentage of good and fair-quality water?
   b) Which two regions have the highest percentage of poor and bad-quality water?
   c) For each region you named in **b)**, suggest a reason why it has a higher than average amount of poor and bad-quality water.

2 Table **E** lists the major types of river pollution.
   a) For each of the first four types, explain how it can cause pollution in rivers.
   b) Complete the table by listing the major causes of pollution in the three named areas.
   c) Why do you think it is difficult to reduce river pollution in the
      i) Rhine   ii) Ganges?

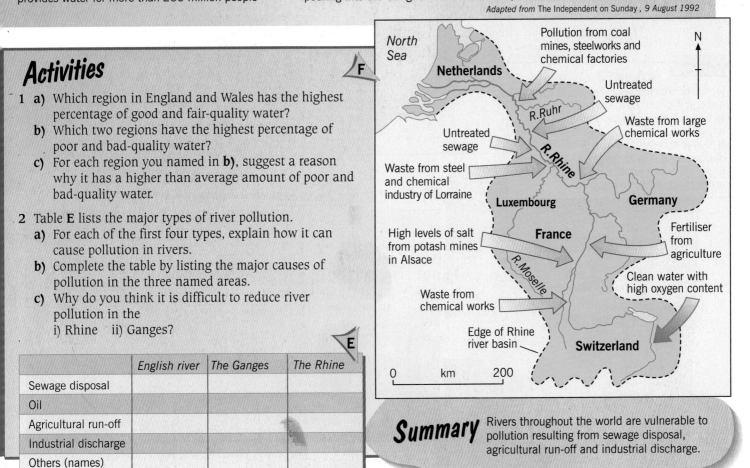

F

North Sea
Netherlands
Pollution from coal mines, steelworks and chemical factories
Untreated sewage
R. Ruhr
Untreated sewage
Waste from large chemical works
Waste from steel and chemical industry of Lorraine
R. Rhine
Luxembourg
Germany
High levels of salt from potash mines in Alsace
France
Fertiliser from agriculture
R. Moselle
Waste from chemical works
Clean water with high oxygen content
Edge of Rhine river basin
Switzerland
0   km   200

E

	English river	The Ganges	The Rhine
Sewage disposal			
Oil			
Agricultural run-off			
Industrial discharge			
Others (names)			

Summary Rivers throughout the world are vulnerable to pollution resulting from sewage disposal, agricultural run-off and industrial discharge.

What are the causes of sea pollution?

In the past, it was believed that the seas were so large and deep that they could not be harmed by human activity. The North Sea has, for centuries, absorbed the waste of North-west Europe. The waste either settled harmlessly on the sea-bed, or was cleansed naturally by the sea. This attitude of 'disperse and dilute' assumed that everything would mix with enough water to become, eventually, harmless.

However, the North Sea is suffering badly from the twin problems of pollution and overfishing. There are limits to the amount of waste that can be put into the sea and to the number of fish that can be taken out. The North Sea is in danger of becoming an empty sea.

Causes of pollution in the North Sea

About 85 per cent of sea pollution comes from land-based activities and 90 per cent of this stays in water near to the coast. The Rhine is responsible for 45 per cent of the river pollutants which enter the North Sea. It collects these as it flows through Switzerland, France, Germany and the Netherlands. Britain is the largest single polluter. Its rivers, mainly the Thames, Tees, Humber and Forth, are responsible for 20 per cent of the total pollutants. The main causes of North Sea pollution are given in diagram **A**. Table **D** shows some of the effects of marine pollution.

A

Rivers
Pollutants reaching a river (page 32) will eventually end up in the sea. This problem is magnified as many rivers flow into the North Sea.
A Agricultural run-off includes fertiliser (nitrate and phosphate) and pesticides.
B Industrial waste includes toxic chemicals and heavy metals. Heavy metals include mercury, zinc, lead and copper. These cannot be broken down by the sea and so they remain on the sea bed or may be taken into the food chain by marine life.

Sewage
A Untreated (raw) sewage, including excrement, condoms and sanitary items. It is piped out to sea but often returns to beaches. Britain alone discharges 1360 million litres a day.
B Sludge dumped at sea, unlike that discharged into rivers (page 32), only needs to be 50 per cent waste water. Sewage sludge contains nitrate and metals.

Oil
Oil can come from ships illegally washing (cleaning) their tanks at sea, from direct dumping, or from accidents (*Braer*, page 131).

Atmospheric pollution
Many air pollutants eventually fall directly into the sea (e.g. as acid rain).

Direct dumping
There are many large settlements next to the coast. People often dump rubbish (glass, plastic, polythene and aluminium containers, as well as litter) into the sea or leave it on beaches. This includes chemical containers accidentally washed overboard.

NORTH SEA

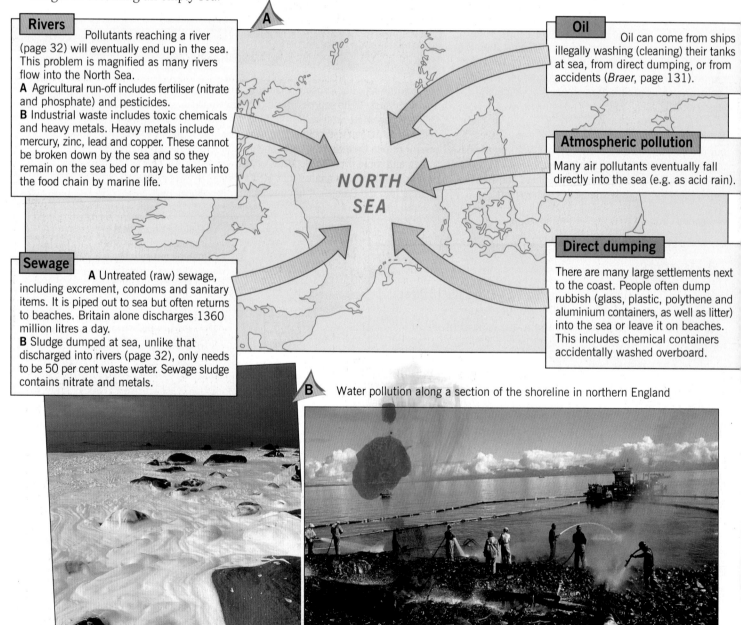

B Water pollution along a section of the shoreline in northern England

C Cleaning oil pollution from the Alaskan coast

D Consequences of pollution in the North Sea

Causes of sea pollution	Effects
Agricultural run-off	Nitrates and phosphate fertiliser cause a build-up of algae. Algae use up oxygen, leaving insufficient for fish and marine life. Pesticides reaching the sea can kill small marine life.
Industrial discharge	Could be a cause for decline in number of mammals (whales and dolphins), and for deformed fish found off British estuaries. Includes metals, e.g. mercury affects the nervous system, and lead causes kidney damage.
Untreated sewage	Visual pollution on beaches. Health risk. Bathers can get stomach upsets, eye infections, skin rashes. In the short term there is a risk of typhoid and salmonella, and a risk of hepatitis and polio in the long term.
Sewage sludge (to end by 1998)	Includes nitrates (agricultural run-off) and metals (industrial discharge). Long-term effects are not known, but it breaks down the sea-bed ecosystem.
Oil	Spoils beaches, kills birds (oil on feathers), fish (oil on gills), shellfish (suffocation) and plankton (cannot photosynthesise).
Atmospheric pollution	Includes radio-active fallout and acid in rainwater.

Activity

Sketch **E** below shows a stretch of coastline bordering the North Sea. It is affected by most of the types of sea pollution described in diagram **A** and table **D**.
- What type of sea pollution is most likely to occur at each of the places numbered **1** to **6** on the sketch?

- What might the effects of sea pollution be on:
  i) the beach at Thorneyhurst
  ii) the Bushell Bird Sanctuary and Nature Reserve
  iii) fish and sea mammals in Stanley Bay?

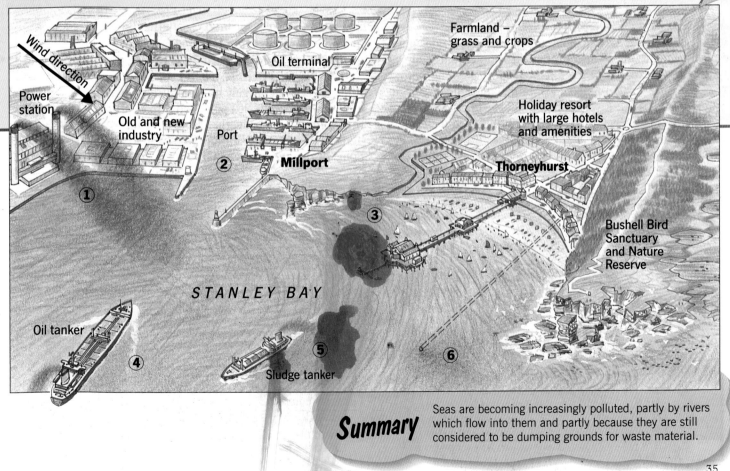

E

Summary Seas are becoming increasingly polluted, partly by rivers which flow into them and partly because they are still considered to be dumping grounds for waste material.

▷ *Where do earthquakes and volcanoes occur?* ◁

One task undertaken by geographers is to plot distributions on maps, and then to see if the maps show any recognisable patterns. Map **A** shows the distribution of world earthquakes and map **B** the distribution of volcanoes. In both cases there are some very obvious patterns.

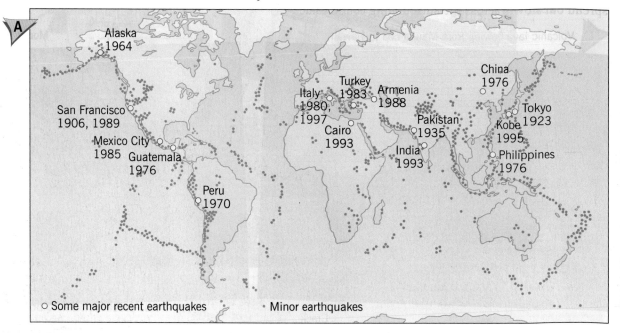

A

Alaska 1964
San Francisco 1906, 1989
Mexico City 1985
Guatemala 1976
Peru 1970
Italy 1980, 1997
Turkey 1983
Armenia 1988
Cairo 1993
Pakistan 1935
India 1993
China 1976
Tokyo 1923
Kobe 1995
Philippines 1976

○ Some major recent earthquakes   · Minor earthquakes

Earthquakes

Earthquakes occur in long narrow belts. The largest belt is the one that goes around the entire Pacific Ocean. The second most obvious is the one that runs through the middle of the Atlantic Ocean for its entire length. A third belt stretches across the continents of Europe and Asia from the Atlantic to the Pacific. There are several other shorter belts, including one going westwards from the west coast of South America.

Volcanoes

Volcanoes also appear in long narrow belts. The largest belt is the one that goes around the entire Pacific Ocean, the so-called 'Pacific Ring of Fire'. The second most obvious is the one that runs through the middle of the Atlantic Ocean for its entire length. Three other notable locations are in southern Europe, the centre of the Pacific Ocean, and eastern Africa.

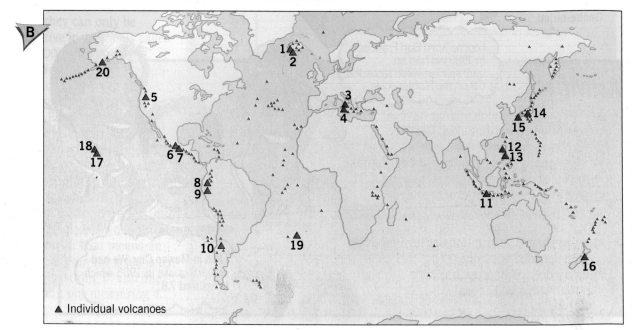

B

1
2
20
5
3
4
18
17
6 7
8
9
10
19
14
15
12
13
11
16

▲ Individual volcanoes

Geographers noticed that when the two maps were laid side by side or, better still, when one was laid on top of the other, earthquakes and volcanoes both seemed to occur in narrow belts and in the same places. These narrow belts are referred to as zones of activity. Having discovered both a pattern and a relationship between the two maps, the geographer then has to ask the question, 'Why?' In this case, why are earthquakes and volcanoes found within the same narrow belts?

Diagram **C** is a cross-section through the Earth. It shows the crust to be the very thin surface layer of cooled rock. It also shows that the crust is not one single piece but is broken into several slabs of varying sizes, called **plates**. Plates float, like rafts, on the molten (semi-solid) mantle. There are two types of crust, and it is important to accept three main differences between them.

- Continental crust is lighter, it cannot sink, and it is permanent (i.e. it is neither renewed nor destroyed).
- Oceanic crust is heavier (denser), it can sink, and it is continually being renewed and destroyed.

Heat from the centre of the Earth sets up convection currents in the mantle (diagram **D**). Where these currents reach the surface they cause the plates above them to move. Most plates only move a few millimetres a year. In some places two plates move towards each other. In others plates may either move apart or pass sideways to each other. A **plate boundary** is where two plates meet. It is at plate boundaries that most of the world's

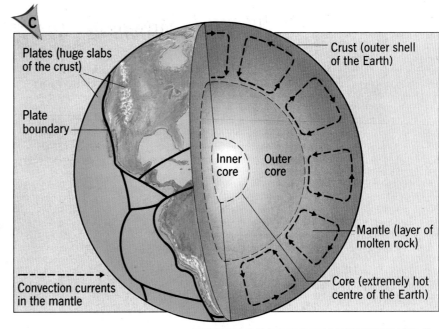

Plates (huge slabs of the crust)

Plate boundary

Crust (outer shell of the Earth)

Inner core

Outer core

Mantle (layer of molten rock)

Core (extremely hot centre of the Earth)

- - - - →
Convection currents in the mantle

C

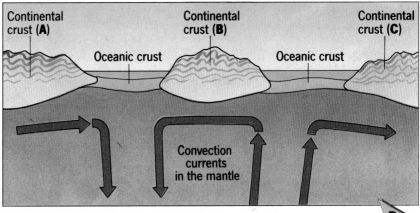

Continental crust (**A**)

Oceanic crust

Continental crust (**B**)

Oceanic crust

Continental crust (**C**)

Convection currents in the mantle

D

earthquakes occur and volcanoes are found (maps **A** and **B**). Pages 54 and 55 explain why there are so many earthquakes and volcanic eruptions, and why some are gentle and others violent, at plate boundaries.

Activities

1 Earthquakes and volcanoes seem to occur in long narrow belts.
   a) Name two belts (areas) where both earthquakes and volcanic eruptions occur.
   b) Name an area in Europe where both earthquakes and volcanic eruptions occur.

2 The following 20 volcanoes have been numbered but not named on map **B**:
   - *Aconcagua* • *Chimborazo* • *Cotopaxi* • *Etna*
   - *Fuji* • *Heimaey* • *Katmai* • *Kilauea*
   - *Krakatoa* • *Mauna Loa* • *Mayon* • *Paricutin*
   - *Pinatubo* • *Popocatapetl* • *Mount St Helens*
   - *Ruapehu* • *Surtsey* • *Tristan da Cunha*
   - *Unzen* • *Vesuvius*.

Pacific Ring of Fire	Middle of oceans	Others
	1 = Heimaey	

E

   a) Name the volcanoes numbered 1 to **20**.
   b) Copy and complete table **E** by giving their locations.

3 **a)** Give three differences between continental crust and oceanic crust.
   b) i) What are plates?
        ii) Why do they move?
        iii) What happens at plate boundaries?
   c) On diagram **D**, what do you think will happen between:
        i) continents **A** and **B**
        ii) continents **B** and **C**?

Summary

The Earth's crust is broken into several plates. Convection currents cause these plates to move about slowly. Earthquakes and volcanic eruptions occur at plate boundaries.

► *What happens at plate boundaries?* ◄

Map **A** shows the major plates and their boundaries (margins). The map key indicates that there are four types of plate boundary – destructive, collision, constructive and conservative. Earthquakes occur at all four types of boundary, but are more violent at some than others. Volcanic eruptions tend to occur at only two types of plate boundary, being violent at one and more gentle at the other.

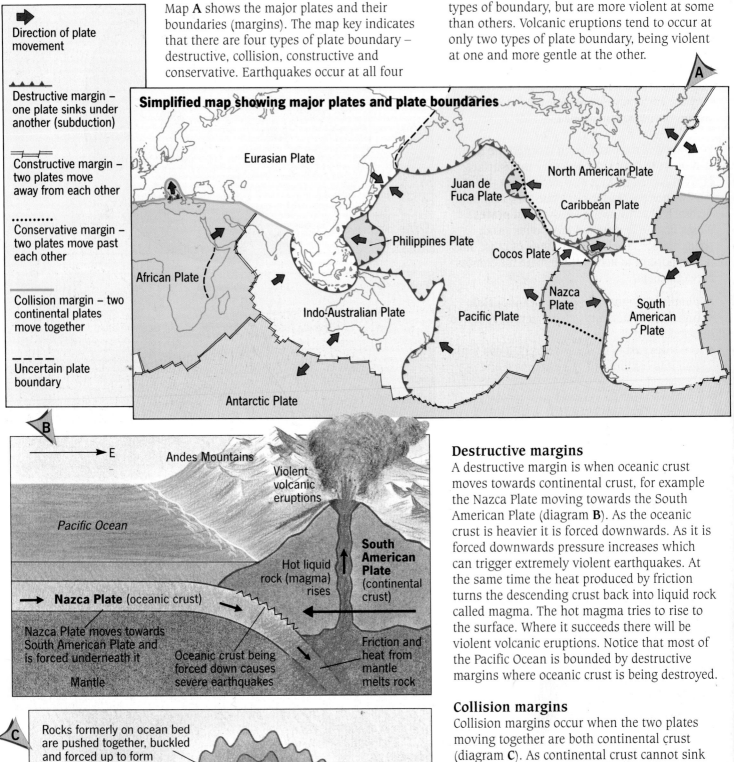

Direction of plate movement

Destructive margin – one plate sinks under another (subduction)

Constructive margin – two plates move away from each other

Conservative margin – two plates move past each other

Collision margin – two continental plates move together

Uncertain plate boundary

A

Simplified map showing major plates and plate boundaries

Eurasian Plate

Juan de Fuca Plate

North American Plate

Caribbean Plate

Philippines Plate

Cocos Plate

African Plate

Nazca Plate

South American Plate

Indo-Australian Plate

Pacific Plate

Antarctic Plate

B

E

Andes Mountains

Violent volcanic eruptions

Pacific Ocean

South American Plate (continental crust)

Hot liquid rock (magma) rises

Nazca Plate (oceanic crust)

Nazca Plate moves towards South American Plate and is forced underneath it

Oceanic crust being forced down causes severe earthquakes

Friction and heat from mantle melts rock

Mantle

C

Rocks formerly on ocean bed are pushed together, buckled and forced up to form Himalayan Mountains

Indo-Australian Plate

Continental crust

Eurasian Plate (almost stationary)

Continental crust

Destructive margins

A destructive margin is when oceanic crust moves towards continental crust, for example the Nazca Plate moving towards the South American Plate (diagram **B**). As the oceanic crust is heavier it is forced downwards. As it is forced downwards pressure increases which can trigger extremely violent earthquakes. At the same time the heat produced by friction turns the descending crust back into liquid rock called magma. The hot magma tries to rise to the surface. Where it succeeds there will be violent volcanic eruptions. Notice that most of the Pacific Ocean is bounded by destructive margins where oceanic crust is being destroyed.

Collision margins

Collision margins occur when the two plates moving together are both continental crust (diagram **C**). As continental crust cannot sink or be destroyed, then the land between them is buckled and pushed upwards to form high 'fold' mountains, such as the Himalayas. Although pressure created by the plates moving together can cause severe earthquakes, there are no volcanic eruptions at collision margins.

Constructive margins

A constructive margin is where two plates move apart, for example the North American Plate moving away from the Eurasian Plate (diagram **D**). As a 'gap' appears between the two plates, then lava can easily escape either in the form of a relatively gentle eruption or as a lava flow. The lava creates new oceanic crust and forms a mid-ocean ridge. While not all earthquakes and volcanic eruptions on Iceland are 'gentle', they are gentle when compared with those at other plate margins.

Conservative margins

At conservative margins two plates try to slide slowly past each other, as in the case of the North American and Pacific Plates (diagram **E**). When the two plates stick, as they often do along the notorious San Andreas Fault in California, pressure builds up. When it is finally released, it creates a severe earthquake. As crust is neither created nor destroyed at conservative margins, there are no volcanic eruptions.

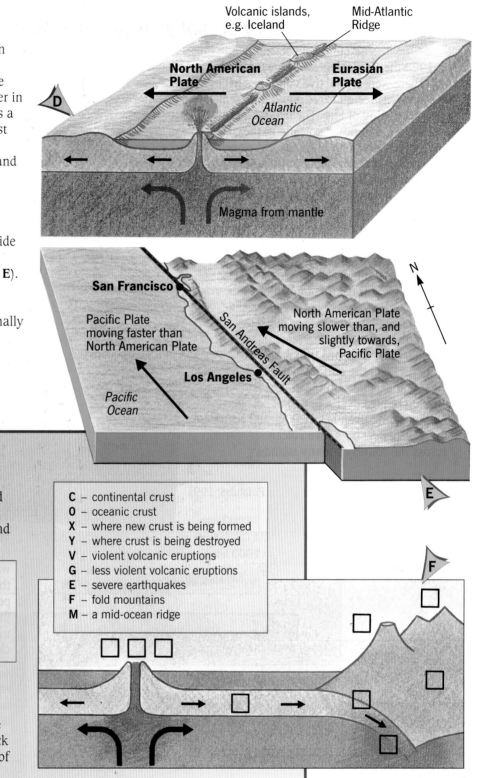

Activities

1 **a)** Describe the differences between destructive, collision, constructive and conservative plate margins.

   b) What type of plate margin can be found between the plates listed below?

   - Nazca and South American
   - North American and Eurasian
   - Nazca and Pacific
   - Indo-Australian and Eurasian
   - North American and Pacific
   - African and Eurasian
   - Pacific and Eurasian

   C – continental crust
   O – oceanic crust
   X – where new crust is being formed
   Y – where crust is being destroyed
   V – violent volcanic eruptions
   G – less violent volcanic eruptions
   E – severe earthquakes
   F – fold mountains
   M – a mid-ocean ridge

2 Make a copy of diagram **F**. Add the appropriate letters to the empty boxes.

3 Copy and complete table **G** by putting one tick in the earthquake column and one tick in the volcanic eruption column for each of the four types of plate boundary.

Plate margin	Earthquakes			Volcanic eruptions		
	Violent	Less violent	Rare	Violent	Fairly gentle	None
Destructive						
Collision						
Constructive						
Passive						

Summary Plates can either move towards, away from or sideways past other plates. The resultant Earth movements can cause earthquakes and volcanic eruptions of differing severity.

▷ Why are people distributed unevenly? ◁

Map **A** is made up from many photos taken from satellites which orbit the Earth. The frozen polar regions and snow-covered mountain ranges stand out white. Forests are green, grasslands a browny-green and deserts a light brown. Red dots have been added to this map to show the distribution of population over the Earth's surface. Although over 5000 million people live in the world, their distribution is very uneven. Most of them are crowded into a third of the land surface, leaving large areas almost uninhabited (graph **B**).

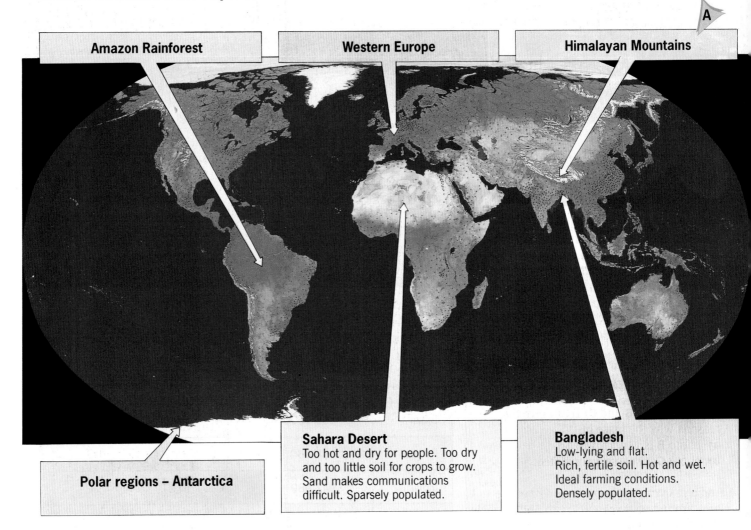

A

Amazon Rainforest

Western Europe

Himalayan Mountains

Polar regions – Antarctica

Sahara Desert
Too hot and dry for people. Too dry and too little soil for crops to grow. Sand makes communications difficult. Sparsely populated.

Bangladesh
Low-lying and flat.
Rich, fertile soil. Hot and wet.
Ideal farming conditions.
Densely populated.

There are many reasons for the different population patterns shown on map **A**. Some of these reasons discourage people from living in an area. These are **negative factors** and result in low population densities. Other reasons encourage people to live in an area. These are **positive factors** and create high population densities. Both the negative and positive factors can be sub-divided into **environmental** (physical) factors and **human** factors.

Negative factors causing low population densities
Environmental factors People are not naturally attracted to areas that have extremes of climate and which are either very cold, very hot, very dry or very wet. Relief discourages settlement especially in areas which have high, steep-sided mountains or are liable to experience volcanic eruptions and earthquakes. The dense coniferous forests and tropical rainforests have relatively few permanent inhabitants. There are also few people living in places where soils are too thin and lack sufficient humus for cultivation or which are experiencing increased erosion caused by deforestation and overgrazing. Areas that lack natural resources such as minerals or energy supplies are less likely to develop industries or to create many jobs. Settlements are less likely to grow in areas that lack a permanent water supply or are troubled by disease and pests.

Human factors Areas that are isolated or where it is difficult to construct and to maintain transport systems are more likely to be sparsely populated. This is also true of places that are a long way inland and away from coasts. Economic causes for low population densities include a lack of wealth and insufficient technology to overcome the environmental factors listed above.

Political decisions by governments may also affect the distribution of population if there is a failure to invest money or to create new settlements with jobs and services.

Positive factors causing high population densities
These factors, mainly a reverse of the negative factors described above, are summarised in diagram **C**.

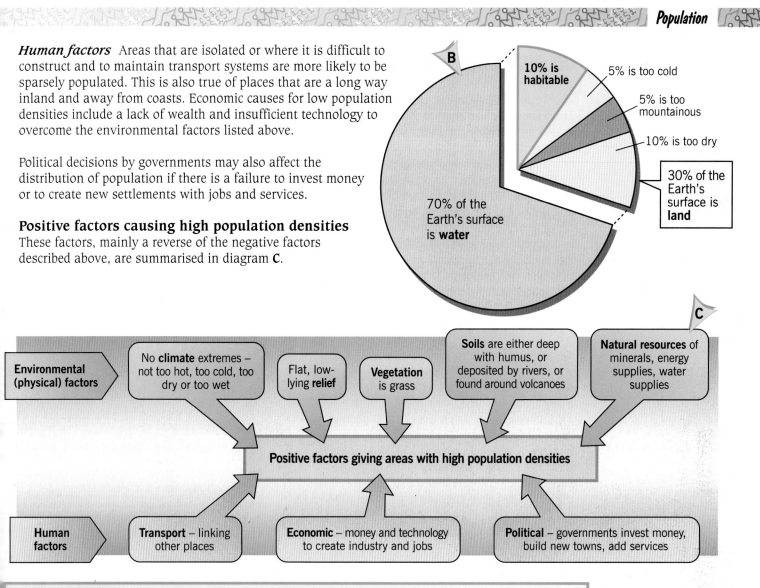

B

10% is habitable
5% is too cold
5% is too mountainous
10% is too dry
30% of the Earth's surface is **land**
70% of the Earth's surface is **water**

C

| Environmental (physical) factors | No **climate** extremes – not too hot, too cold, too dry or too wet | Flat, low-lying **relief** | **Vegetation** is grass | **Soils** are either deep with humus, or deposited by rivers, or found around volcanoes | **Natural resources** of minerals, energy supplies, water supplies |

Positive factors giving areas with high population densities

| Human factors | **Transport** – linking other places | **Economic** – money and technology to create industry and jobs | **Political** – governments invest money, build new towns, add services |

Activities

1 Map **A** names six parts of the world that have either a high or a low population density. Two of these areas have been described on the map. For each of the remaining four regions:
   a) state whether its population density is high or low
   b) give as many reasons as possible why its population density is high or low.

2 Choose one area in the world with a high population density and one with a low population density. Choose **different** places to those named on map **A**. Copy and complete diagram **D** by adding information from your chosen areas.

3 What negative factors and what positive factors have affected the density of population in your home region?

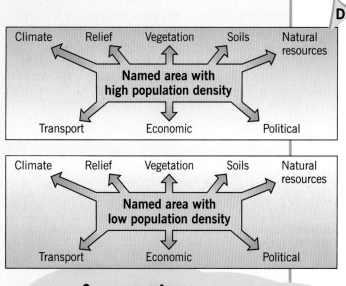

D

Climate Relief Vegetation Soils Natural resources
Named area with high population density
Transport Economic Political

Climate Relief Vegetation Soils Natural resources
Named area with low population density
Transport Economic Political

Summary

People are not spread evenly throughout the world. Negative factors discourage settlement, giving low population densities, while positive factors encourage settlement, creating high population densities.

How do birth and death rates affect population growth?

The world's population is growing very rapidly. This is because the number of babies born each year is greatly exceeding the number of people who are dying. In 1995 the United Nations estimated that the world's total population of 5718 million was increasing by 90 million a year – more than the combined present populations of the UK and Canada. If this trend continues, the world's population could double by the year 2150 (graph **A**). This rapid growth has been called 'a population explosion'. However, this explosion is not evenly distributed, as 97 per cent of the increase will take place in the three developing continents of Africa, Asia and South America.

The major reason for population changes, whether in a particular country or for the whole world, is the change in **birth rates** and **death rates**. The birth rate is the number of live babies born in a year for every 1000 people in the total population. The death rate is the number of people in every 1000 who die each year. The **natural increase** is the difference between the birth rate and the death rate. If the birth rate is higher then the total population will increase (diagram **B**). If the death rate is higher then the total population will decrease.

Birth rates and death rates for all countries change over periods of time. Through the study of many countries a **model** can be made to show population changes. This model is called the **demographic transition model**. A model is used to simplify difficult real world situations to make them easier to understand. The demographic transition model suggests

that population changes for all countries go through four stages. Diagram **C** shows these stages and gives some of the reasons why many of the less economically developed countries are in Stage 2, while the more economically developed countries have reached Stage 4. Recently several West European countries appear to have reached a new and fifth stage where death rates are exceeding birth rates.

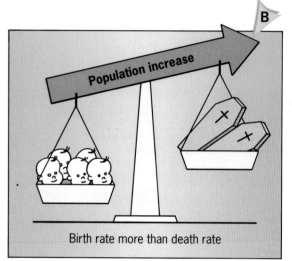

B

Population increase

Birth rate more than death rate

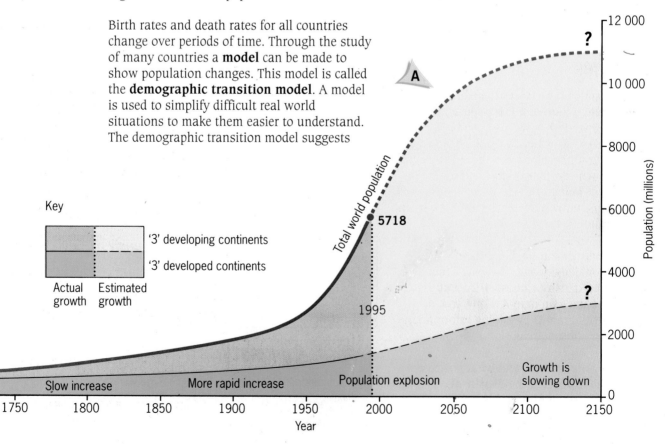

A

Key

'3' developing continents

'3' developed continents

Actual growth | Estimated growth

Total world population

5718

1995

Slow increase | More rapid increase | Population explosion | Growth is slowing down

1750   1800   1850   1900   1950   2000   2050   2100   2150

Year

12 000
10 000
8000
6000
4000
2000
0

Population (millions)

C

Stage	1 High stationary	2 Early expanding	3 Late expanding	4 Low stationary	5? Declining?

Graph — Birth and death rates (per 1000 people per year): axis marked 0, 10, 20, 30, 40. Lines labelled Death rate, Birth rate, Total population, Natural increase, Natural decrease. Markers "?" in stage 5.

	1 High stationary	2 Early expanding	3 Late expanding	4 Low stationary	5? Declining?
Examples	A few remote groups	Egypt, Kenya, India	Brazil	USA, Japan, France, UK	Germany, Italy
Birth rate	High	High	Falling	Low	Very low
Death rate	High	Falls rapidly	Falls more slowly	Low	Low
Natural increase	Stable or slow increase	Very rapid increase	Increase slows down	Stable or slow increase	Slow decrease
Reasons for changes in birth rate	Many children needed for farming. Many children die at an early age. Religious/social encouragement. No family planning.		Improved medical care and diet. Fewer children needed.	Family planning. Good health. Improving status of women. Later marriages.	
Reasons for changes in death rate	Disease, famine. Poor medical knowledge so many children die.	Improvements in medical care, water supply and sanitation. Fewer children die.		Good health care. Reliable food supply.	

Activities

1 a) What was the world's population when you were born?
   b) What will it be on your 18th and 60th birthdays?
   c) What was the world's population in 1995?
   d) How many years will it take for that population to double?
   e) Complete diagram **D** to show how rapidly the world's population is increasing.

2 What is meant by each of the following terms:
   • *birth rate*
   • *death rate*
   • *natural increase*?

3 a) Name a developing country which you have studied.
   b) Why does it have a high birth rate?
   c) Why is its death rate still high but beginning to fall?
   d) Name a developed country which you have studied.
   e) Why does it have a low birth rate and a low death rate?
   f) In which stage of the demographic transition model are each of your chosen countries?

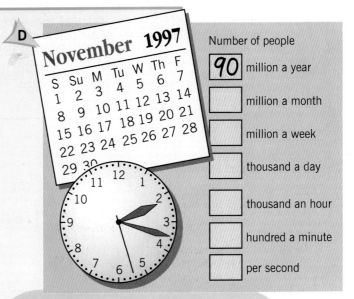

D

November 1997

S	Su	M	Tu	W	Th	F
	1	2	3	4	5	6	7
	8	9	10	11	12	13	14
	15	16	17	18	19	20	21
	22	23	24	25	26	27	28
	29	30

Number of people

90	million a year
	million a month
	million a week
	thousand a day
	thousand an hour
	hundred a minute
	per second

Summary Population growth depends upon changes in birth and death rates. Changes in a country's population seem to pass through several stages known as the demographic transition.

Why do birth and death rates differ?

It has already been suggested that the birth rates, death rates and natural increases differ between developed and developing countries. Likewise, there are differences between **infant mortality rates** and **life expectancy**. Infant mortality is the number of children out of every 1000 born alive who die before they reach the age of one year. Life expectancy is the average number of years a person born in a country can expect to live. As table **A** shows, developing countries have high birth rates, high infant mortality rates, rapid population growth and a relatively short life expectancy. Due to high birth rates in developing countries, most people in every 1000 are younger than 15 and there are relatively few elderly people. Death rates are high but appear low compared with the huge numbers living. As countries develop economically and become more wealthy this pattern is reversed.

A

Country (1994)	Birth rate	Death rate	Natural increase	Infant mortality rate	Life expectancy
Kenya	47	10	37	64	61
Bangladesh	41	14	27	108	53
India	31	10	21	88	62
Egypt	31	9	22	57	62
Brazil	26	8	18	57	66

Country (1994)	Birth rate	Death rate	Natural increase	Infant mortality rate	Life expectancy
USA	14	9	5	8	76
UK	14	12	2	8	76
France	13	10	3	7	77
Japan	12	8	4	5	79
Germany	11	12	−1	8	75

Differences in birth and death rates

B

Developing countries, e.g. India
Birth rates are high often because people want and need large families. The relatively short life expectancy is more likely to result from a lack of wealth.

C

Developed countries, e.g. UK
Birth rates are low often because people do not need many children and prefer small families. The longer life expectancy results from the greater amount of wealth that is available.

Why a high birth rate?

Why a short life expectancy?

We need many children:
- to help us work on the land and to carry wood and water,
- to care for us when we are ill or old and cannot work,
- because so many die from disease. Four of my eight children died before their first birthday.

Both my parents died when they were quite young. My mother died during a famine. My father caught cholera from dirty water. There was no hospital near and we could not afford medical care.

One child might get a job in the city and send us money

My religion forbids birth control

Having a big family increases my importance in the village.

Why a long life expectancy?

Why a low birth rate?

Both my parents are still alive. They live near to a doctor and a hospital. Their home has central heating. They are very comfortable.

Family planning controls the size of our family.

We only wanted two children and we are sure they will live a long life, free from disease.

We can afford to spend more money on our car, holidays and entertainment .

We have pensions for when we are old.

I wanted to return to my career and not stay at home.

How can birth rates be reduced?

The demographic transition model on page 67 shows death rates falling before birth rates. This suggests that birth rates are the harder of the two to lower. Yet it is essential that poorer countries, like India, do lower their birth rates (extract **D**). However, many of them seem a long way from imitating some of the methods that have proved to be successful in the better-off developed countries.

The United Nations state that there are two basic needs which must be accepted if birth rates are to be controlled:

1 To improve the status of women and to realise that they have the right (not accepted in many countries) to make the decision between having more children, or birth control.

2 To provide further education, especially for women, on family planning.

A lesser, but still important, need is to try to reduce poverty. It was previously believed that high birth rates were a result of poverty. However, in those parts of the world where the status of women has been raised, there has been a decline in the birth rate even though there has been no obvious reduction in poverty (extract **D**).

D

Birth control in India

In the minute of time that a motorist has to wait for a red traffic light to change colour, another 35 babies will have been born in Calcutta or Bombay in India. In London the motorist might miss the green light waiting for a birth in Britain. Unless India can reduce its birth rate its population will exceed 2 billion, and that of China's, by 2035. India's population control efforts so far have failed. The aim was to have two children per family by the year 2000, but the figures so far are double that.

Social workers have found the best contraceptive not to be condoms, the Pill, or sterilisation, but female literacy. Couples living in high literacy states, especially those where girls have also had an education, tend to have only two children. In the more populous states where fewer can read, families still have more than five children.

A better deal for women

Reduced poverty

Better education, especially for women

Family planning

Later marriages

Improved health

E

Activities

1 What is meant by the terms *infant mortality rate* and *life expectancy*?

2 a) Give four reasons why many families in developing countries are large, with five or more children.
   b) Give four reasons why many families in developed countries are small, with no more than two children.

3 a) How can birth rates be reduced? Use extract **D** and diagram to help you.
   b) Why is it difficult for countries like India to reduce the birth rate?
   c) Design a poster showing the need for family planning for a small village in a developing country where few of the people can read or write.

Summary

Developing countries have higher birth and infant mortality rates than developed countries. Birth rates may only fall when the status of women and the standard of education improves.

What are the problems of urbanisation?

Cities in developing countries

The term **urbanisation** means the increase in the proportion of the world's population who live in cities. Urbanisation has increased rapidly in developed countries since the mid-nineteenth century and in developing countries since the mid-twentieth century (table **A**). Between 1950 and 1995 the urban population in developing countries more than doubled (100+ per cent increase). In developed countries the increase was less than half. Apart from urbanisation there have been two other rapid changes (map **B**).

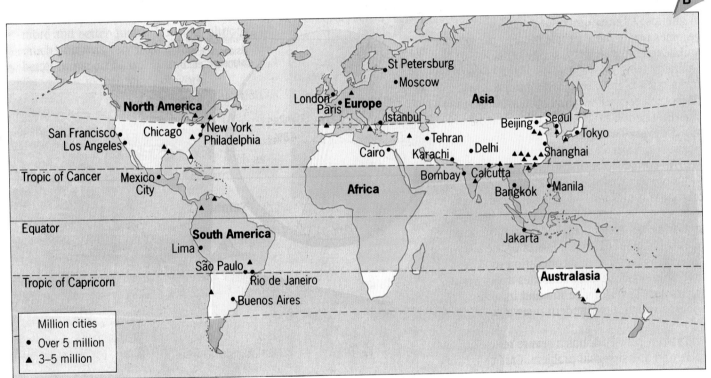

A

	1950	*1995*
World	30%	53%
Developed countries	53%	74%
Developing countries	17%	37%

1 The increase in **million cities**, i.e. places with over one million inhabitants. In 1850 the only two million cities in the world were London and Paris. By 1990 there were 286.

2 The increase in million cities located in developing countries, especially within the tropics.

B

North America · St Petersburg · Moscow · London · Paris · Europe · Istanbul · Asia · San Francisco · Chicago · New York · Philadelphia · Los Angeles · Tehran · Beijing · Seoul · Tokyo · Cairo · Karachi · Delhi · Shanghai · Tropic of Cancer · Mexico City · Bombay · Calcutta · Africa · Bangkok · Manila · Equator · South America · Lima · Jakarta · São Paulo · Rio de Janeiro · Tropic of Capricorn · Buenos Aires · Australasia

Million cities
- Over 5 million
▲ 3–5 million

What are the problems of rapid urbanisation? A case study of Calcutta

Calcutta is a good example of how problems are created when cities grow too quickly. The city is built on flat, swampy land alongside the River Hooghly which is part of the Ganges Delta. Its population is believed to have grown from 7 million in 1970 to over 13 million in 1995. As Calcutta has a high birth rate and receives many migrants from the surrounding rural areas, it is claimed that its population will exceed 16 million by the year 2000. The city authorities have no hope of providing enough new homes, jobs or services for the increasing population.

Housing Many families have no homes and have to live on pavements (photo **C**). Nearly half a million people are reported to sleep in the open, covered only by bamboo matting, sacking, polythene or newspaper. Many more live in shanty settlements called, in India, bustees. Bustee houses have mud floors, wattle or wooden walls, and tiled or corrugated iron roofs – materials which are not the best for giving protection against the heavy monsoon rains. The houses are packed closely together and are separated by narrow alleys (photo **D**). Inside each house there is probably only one small room, in which the whole family, perhaps up to ten in number, live, eat and sleep.

Services Houses lack electricity, running water and sewage disposal. There are very few schools and a lack of doctors and hospitals. Public transport is often absent or overcrowded.

C Pavement dwellers, Calcutta

D A lane in the bustees

Sanitation and health One water tap and one toilet in each alley may serve up to 50 people. Sewage often flows down the alley and may contaminate drinking water causing cholera, typhoid and dysentery. Rubbish, dumped in the streets, provides an ideal breeding ground for disease. Most children have worms and suffer from malnutrition.

Employment Those with jobs often use their homes as a place of work. The front of the house can be 'opened up' to allow the occupants to sell food, wood, clothes and household utensils (photo **E**). Few people in the bustees are totally unemployed, but most jobs only occupy a few hours a week.

Crime This is a major problem as people struggle to survive and as there is not enough money to try to prevent crime or catch criminals.

The Calcutta Metropolitan Development Agency, set up in 1970, has tried to make the bustees more habitable by paving alleys, digging drains, and providing more water taps and toilets. Pre-fabricated houses have been built and a better community atmosphere created. Even so, the lack of money has meant only relatively small areas have been improved.

E Spices stall in a Calcutta bustee

Activities

1 **a)** What is meant by *urbanisation*?
  b) Give three points to describe the distribution of million cities.

2 **a)** Describe the scenes in photos **C**, **D** and **E**. Mention the houses, the alleys and jobs.
  b) What do you consider to be the worst problems of living in the bustees?

Summary Urbanisation is the increase in the proportion of people living in cities. It is most rapid in cities in developing countries where it causes considerable problems.

8 Urban patterns and changes
▶ Is there a typical land use pattern? ◀

It has been suggested that towns and cities do not grow in a haphazard way but tend to develop recognisable shapes and patterns. Although each town is unique and will have developed its own distinctive pattern making it different from other towns, it will also show some characteristics shared by other urban settlements. Several people have offered theories as to how these characteristic patterns and shapes develop. These theories are illustrated as **urban land use models**. Remember that a model is used to simplify complex real world situations and make them easier to explain and to understand. The two simplest models are shown in diagram **A**.

The Burgess model Burgess claimed that the focal point of a town was the **central business district** or **CBD**. As towns developed they grew outwards from the CBD. This means that buildings become increasingly more recent towards the city boundary. The outward growth is shown on the model by four circular zones. Apart from the transition zone next to the CBD, where Burgess suggested industry had replaced the oldest of houses, the resultant circular zones were based on the age of the houses and the wealth of their occupants.

The Hoyt model By the time Hoyt suggested his model, public transport had become much more important. Just as older factories grew up alongside canals and railways, so newer industries located along main roads leading out of cities. As a result Hoyt suggested that towns developed in sectors, or as wedge shapes, along main transport routes. Hoyt also claimed that if industry and low-cost housing grew in one part of a town in the nineteenth century, then newer industries and modern low-cost housing would also develop in that same sector.

Functional zones in a city

As towns continued to grow, each of the zones shown on diagram **A** developed its own special type of land use. Each type of land use performs a special **function** or purpose. The three major types of land use, or functions, in a town are shops and offices, industry, and housing (photo **B**). Other types of land use include parks, transport and services. It has already been pointed out that each city will develop its own pattern of land use, and that

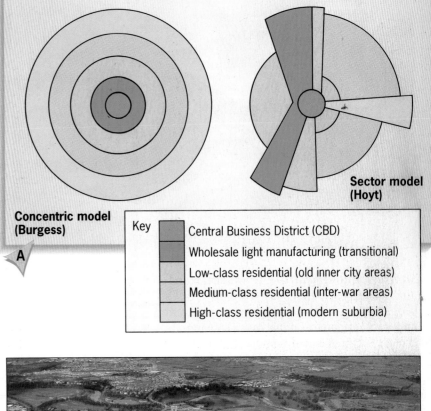

Concentric model (Burgess)

Sector model (Hoyt)

Key	
	Central Business District (CBD)
	Wholesale light manufacturing (transitional)
	Low-class residential (old inner city areas)
	Medium-class residential (inter-war areas)
	High-class residential (modern suburbia)

A

B Land use zones in a city: Carlisle

each pattern will be more complex than that shown in the Burgess and Hoyt models. Diagram **C** is a more realistic map showing land use and functional zones in a city.

Land use and functional zones

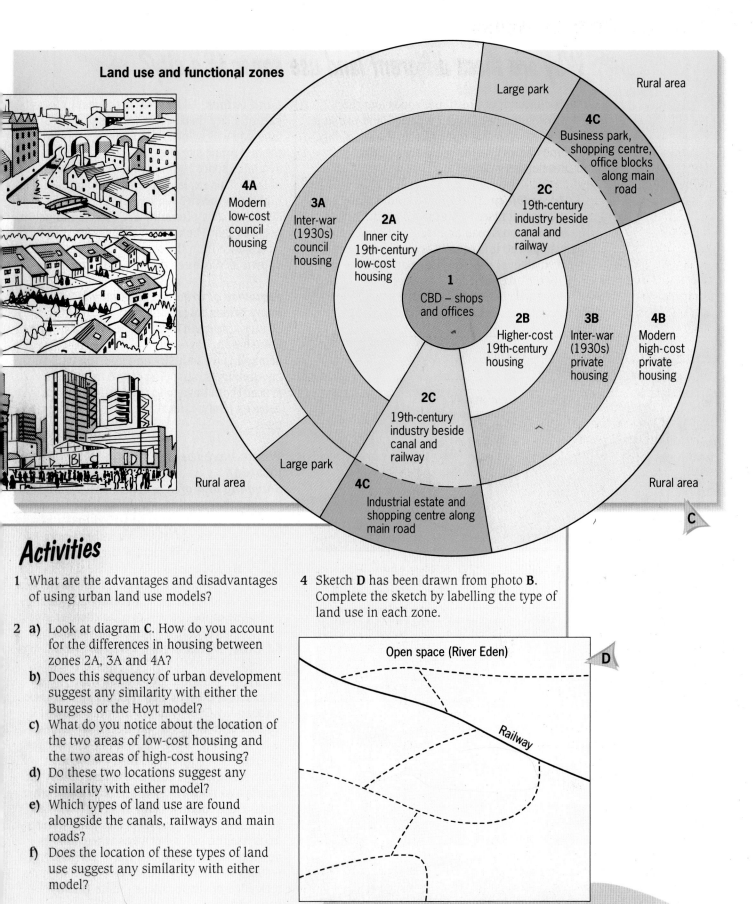

4A Modern low-cost council housing

3A Inter-war (1930s) council housing

2A Inner city 19th-century low-cost housing

1 CBD – shops and offices

Large park

Rural area

4C Business park, shopping centre, office blocks along main road

2C 19th-century industry beside canal and railway

2B Higher-cost 19th-century housing

3B Inter-war (1930s) private housing

4B Modern high-cost private housing

Rural area

2C 19th-century industry beside canal and railway

4C Industrial estate and shopping centre along main road

Large park

Rural area

C

Activities

1 What are the advantages and disadvantages of using urban land use models?

2 **a)** Look at diagram **C**. How do you account for the differences in housing between zones 2A, 3A and 4A?

b) Does this sequence of urban development suggest any similarity with either the Burgess or the Hoyt model?

c) What do you notice about the location of the two areas of low-cost housing and the two areas of high-cost housing?

d) Do these two locations suggest any similarity with either model?

e) Which types of land use are found alongside the canals, railways and main roads?

f) Does the location of these types of land use suggest any similarity with either model?

3 Match the three sketches in diagram **C** to their appropriate zones.

4 Sketch **D** has been drawn from photo **B**. Complete the sketch by labelling the type of land use in each zone.

Open space (River Eden)

D

Railway

Summary It is possible to recognise patterns of land use and functional zones within a city. These patterns can be shown more simply as urban land use models.

Why are there different land use zones in a city?

The location of functional zones and the distribution of different types of land use in a city are related to three factors – accessibility, land values and the sequence of urban development.

Accessibility The CBD has traditionally been the easiest place in the city to reach. This is because most road and local rail routes meet here and so it is equally accessible to people from all over the city. Places on the edge of a city are accessible for local people but not to those who live on the opposite side of that urban area.

A

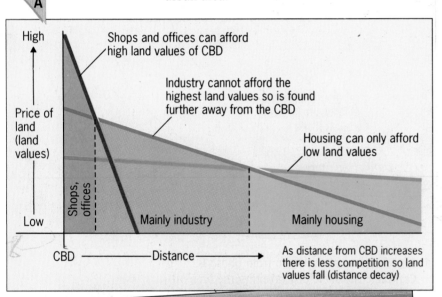

High

Price of land (land values)

Low

Shops and offices can afford high land values of CBD

Industry cannot afford the highest land values so is found further away from the CBD

Housing can only afford low land values

Shops, offices

Mainly industry

Mainly housing

CBD ——— Distance ———➤

As distance from CBD increases there is less competition so land values fall (distance decay)

Land values As the CBD is the most accessible part of a city then several different types of land use will want to locate here. Competition for this prime site, especially as the amount of available space is limited, pushes up the price of land. This explains why land values are highest in the city centre. As competition decreases away from the CBD, then land values begin to fall. The concept of land values falling as distance from the city centre increases is known as **distance decay** (diagram **A**).

Sequence of urban development When many British towns began to expand last century, the main demand for land came from industry and low-cost housing. Present-day demand is for industry and housing in pleasant environments, shopping centres and open space. These have to locate on the edges of cities as land nearer the centre has already been used.

Where have the main types of land use located?

Shopping and offices These locate in the CBD because they need to be accessible to as many people as possible. They are often found in high-rise buildings which gives them more space and helps to offset the high cost of land (photo **B**). Even so, it is only those shops and commercial companies making high profits that can afford to locate here. Recently many shops and some offices have moved to cheaper land on the edge of cities, especially if those sites have easy access to good roads and motorways.

Industry Until the growth of industry most cities did not extend beyond the limits of their present-day CBD. When industry developed it located next to the city centre on the nearest available land. Being the first in the sequence of urban development, industry located on what was then the edge of the city. Nearby canals and railways gave accessibility to other parts of the country. Later urban growth has meant that what remains of this early industry finds itself in inner city areas where land is now expensive and where traffic congestion reduces accessibility (photo **C**). New industries seek edge-of-city locations (photo **D** and page 139).

B London's financial district

Housing In the last century people lived in tightly-packed housing within walking distance of their places of work, which were either in the city centre or in the local factory (photo **E**). During the twentieth century a sequence of housing developments has taken place (photos **F** and **G**). Improved public and private transport has increased people's mobility. Recent housing developments have therefore taken place a long way from the city centre. As land values are lower here, many houses are large and have easy access to open space.

C

D

E

G

Activities

1 Table **H** lists the three main types of land use in a city. On an enlarged copy show how the location of these types of land use have been affected by accessibility, land values and the sequence of urban development.

H

Land use		Location	Accessibility	Land values	Sequence of urban development
Shops and offices					
Industry	19th century				
	Modern				
Housing	19th century				
	Recent				

2 The six photos (labelled **B** to **G**) show different types of land use in a city in Britain. Although the photos were not taken in Carlisle they do show the same type of land use found at the following map references on pages 82 and 83:
- 387592
- 395586
- 401559
- 398577
- 399553
- 408553

Complete table **I** by matching each map reference with the correct photo.

I

Photo	Map reference
B	
C	
D	
E	
F	
G	

Summary

The location of functional zones and the distribution of land use in a city are affected by accessibility, land values and the sequence of urban development.

Why does land use in a city change?

Settlements are constantly changing. As towns and cities develop, or decline, their layout, land use and functions are all likely to alter. These changes, the result of human actions and decisions, have various effects on different groups of people living in a town or city. Changes in land use can result from several processes. These include:

- the ageing of parts of the city
- the decline of original economic activities and their replacement by newer economic activities
- changes in people's needs and expectations, especially their attitudes to living conditions
- increased concern for the environment.

How have processes of change affected land use in inner cities?

British towns began to grow rapidly at the beginning of the Industrial Revolution in the early nineteenth century. The first developments took place in areas next to the city centre – places now referred to as inner city areas. Large factories were built and houses were built as close as possible to them (map **A** and photo **B**). This enabled the factory workers, who had no other form of transport in those days, to walk to work easily. As house builders were not subject to building regulations they tried to pack as many houses into as small an area as possible (photo **C**). It was usual for a factory to be found at one end of a street and either a corner shop or a public house at the other. Most factories were built beside canals or railways. No land was wasted, and was too valuable to be left as open space.

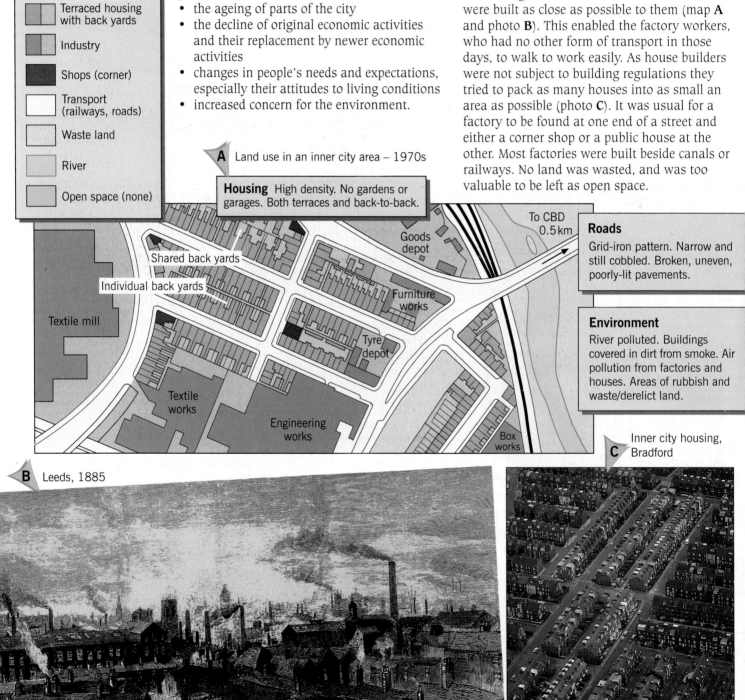

Key

- Terraced housing with back yards
- Industry
- Shops (corner)
- Transport (railways, roads)
- Waste land
- River
- Open space (none)

A Land use in an inner city area – 1970s

Housing High density. No gardens or garages. Both terraces and back-to-back.

Shared back yards

Individual back yards

Textile mill

Goods depot

Furniture works

Tyre depot

Textile works

Engineering works

Box works

To CBD 0.5 km

Roads Grid-iron pattern. Narrow and still cobbled. Broken, uneven, poorly-lit pavements.

Environment River polluted. Buildings covered in dirt from smoke. Air pollution from factories and houses. Areas of rubbish and waste/derelict land.

C Inner city housing, Bradford

B Leeds, 1885

Why did many inner cities decline?

Industry declined as old factories closed down either due to their age, competition from new products, congested sites with insufficient room to expand, poor transport facilities with canals and railways closed and roads narrow and congested, or because of the area's unattractive environment. Some factories remained empty and have decayed while others were pulled down and the land often left unused.

Housing in many cities had become slum-like by the 1960s, often through no fault of the occupants. Many houses were already a hundred years old and built before such amenities as electricity, running water, indoor toilets and damp courses were considered to be essential or had become available (photo **D** and graph **E**).

The **environment** was polluted and unattractive. Houses were blackened by smoke from factory and domestic chimneys, and Clean Air Acts were still a thing of the future. Rivers and canals were a dumping ground for industrial and household waste. Empty buildings were vandalised while sites of demolished buildings became rubbish tips.

How did this decline affect people?

People living in inner city areas wanted:

- Jobs. The original factories employed hundreds of manual and unskilled workers. When these factories closed down there was little alternative work and much unemployment.
- Better housing with modern amenities.
- Things to do in their leisure time. A lack of indoor and outdoor recreational facilities increased boredom and is blamed for a rise in crime among the younger age group.
- A cleaner and a more attractive environment.

D

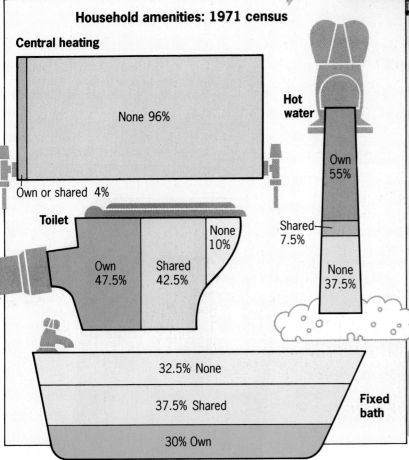

E

Household amenities: 1971 census

Central heating

None 96%

Own or shared 4%

Toilet

Own 47.5% Shared 42.5% None 10%

Hot water

Own 55%

Shared 7.5%

None 37.5%

32.5% None

37.5% Shared

30% Own

Fixed bath

Activities

1 **a)** What were the three major types of land use in an old inner city area?
   b) Which important type of land use was often absent in old inner city areas?

2 **a)** Describe the likely living conditions in areas such as those in photos **B**, **C** and **D**.
   b) List some ways in which you think these areas could have been improved.

3 Think of your local town or city. What changes have you seen take place:
   a) in the CBD (city centre)
   b) in inner city areas next to the CBD
   c) on the edges of the town or city?

Summary

Land use and functions change as settlements get older and people develop different needs. One example is the inner city where changes in land use have affected different groups of people.

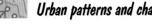
How has land use changed in London's Docklands?

During the nineteenth century the port of London was the busiest in the world. The docks were surrounded by:

- warehouses storing goods being brought into or sent out of Britain
- industries using imported goods
- high-density, poor-quality housing (map **A**).

After the 1950s the size of ships increased so much that they could no longer reach London's docks. By 1970 Docklands had become virtually derelict with few jobs, few amenities, and poor living conditions for the local people (photo **B**). In 1981 the London Docklands Development Corporation (LDDC) was set up to try to improve the economic, social and environmental conditions of the area.

A What were conditions and land use like in 1981?

Housing High-density housing covered most of the area not used by industry. Houses were small and lacked modern amenities but were cheap enough for poorly paid workers to afford, and created a strong 'East Enders' community.

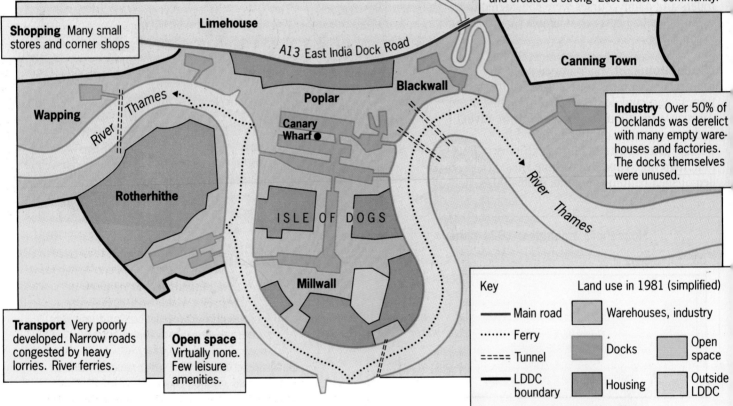

Shopping Many small stores and corner shops

Limehouse

A13 East India Dock Road

Canning Town

Blackwall

Poplar

Wapping

River Thames

Canary Wharf ●

Industry Over 50% of Docklands was derelict with many empty warehouses and factories. The docks themselves were unused.

Rotherhithe

ISLE OF DOGS

River Thames

Millwall

Transport Very poorly developed. Narrow roads congested by heavy lorries. River ferries.

Open space Virtually none. Few leisure amenities.

Key — Land use in 1981 (simplified)
- —— Main road
- ···· Ferry
- ===== Tunnel
- —— LDDC boundary
- Warehouses, industry
- Docks
- Housing
- Open space
- Outside LDDC

How did these conditions affect the local people?

Traditional jobs in the docks and nearby industries had been manual, unskilled, unreliable and poorly paid. By 1981 large numbers of local people were unemployed and living in sub-standard housing in a poor-quality environment. Many were forced to leave the area to look for work and a better quality of life elsewhere.

These were the conditions when the LDDC was set up. It was given three main tasks:

1. To improve economic conditions by creating more jobs and improving the transport system both to and within the area.
2. To improve the environment by restoring derelict land, cleaning up the docks and creating areas of open space.
3. To improve social conditions by creating new housing and recreational amenities, and improving shopping facilities.

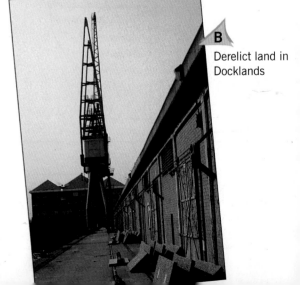

B Derelict land in Docklands

How had land use changed by the mid-1990s?

Industry Many new office blocks had been built including that at Canary Wharf (photo **C**). Financial businesses and high-tech firms were attracted by the low rates, and several large newspaper organisations moved here from their expensive sites in the centre of London. Over 10 000 jobs had been created before the recession of 1992.

Housing Approximately 20 000 new houses and flats had been built. Many old warehouses overlooking the River Thames had been converted into luxury flats. Elsewhere lower-cost housing with modern amenities had replaced most of the older properties (photo **C**).

Transport Improved transport links have brought the Docklands within 10 minutes of central London. The City Airport, built between two docks, and the Dockland Light Railway both opened in 1987. Roads have been improved. The Jubilee underground line is being extended into the Docklands.

Shopping Improved shopping facilities include large superstores near to Canary Wharf and at Surrey Quays, and a luxury complex at Tobacco Wharf.

Environment and recreation facilities The environment has benefited from Europe's largest urban tree planting scheme and the setting up of 17 conservation areas. Recreational additions include a national indoor sports centre and improved amenities for water sports.

C Canary Wharf

How have people been affected by these changes?

Many of the new firms needed highly skilled people but in relatively small numbers. This meant that most new jobs went to people living outside of Docklands. As much of the new housing was expensive it was beyond the reach of local people. This led to well-off people moving in but they rarely mixed with the original 'East Enders'. Recently, more low-cost housing has been built and more local people have been able to buy their own home. While wealthy newcomers have brought extra money and trade into the area, they have caused local shop and recreational prices to rise. Money has been spent on expensive office blocks and houses rather than on improving local services such as hospitals and care for the elderly. By 1990 it was believed that the economic and environmental conditions had improved but not the social conditions.

Activities

1 Table **D** refers to London's Docklands. Copy and complete it to:
   a) summarise the changes in land use between 1981 and the early 1990s
   b) show which groups of people benefited or lost out as a result of the changes.

2 Why is it believed that since 1981 economic and environmental conditions have improved in this area but social conditions have not?

D

Land use 1981	Land use today	Groups in favour of change	Groups against the changes

Summary

The London Docklands is an example of how land use in an inner city area has changed. The changes have greatly affected the lives of people living there.

9 Transport

What are transport networks?

A transport **network**, or system, is when several places are joined together by a series of routes to form a pattern. Transport networks vary both within a country and between countries. A network consists of two elements:

1 **Links** are the routes between places.
2 **Nodes** are places where two or more routes meet (diagram **A**).

The transport pattern produced also shows the accessibility of a place and the density of the network. **Accessibility** is the ease by which one place may be reached from other places. On diagram **A**, place J has the greatest accessibility as it is connected to all of the other places. Place W is the least accessible as it is only directly connected to one other place. **Density** shows the number of routes and how closely packed together they are (diagram **B**). The network density is found by dividing the total length of the routes within an area by the size of area in which those routes are found. For example, on diagram **B (ii)**:

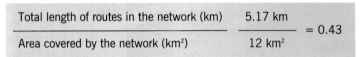

Total length of routes in the network (km)	5.17 km	
Area covered by the network (km²)	12 km²	= 0.43

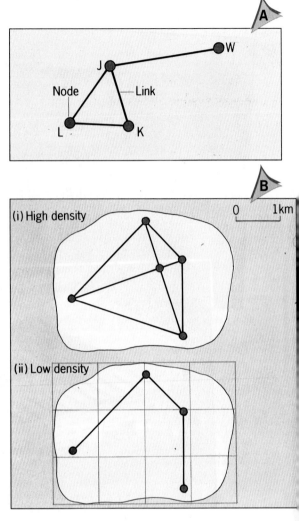

Notice that an area with a high density has more links and nodes and that places within the network are more accessible than those in an area which has a low density.

How do road and rail networks compare in Britain?

Diagram **C** is taken from the OS map on pages 82 and 83. It shows, in common with elsewhere in Britain, that:

- the road network has a higher density than the rail network
- both networks have a higher density in the urban area than in the surrounding rural areas.

What the diagram does not show is that the highest densities in Britain are in the south and east where most people live, where there is more wealth to build routes, and where the land is flatter and more low-lying.

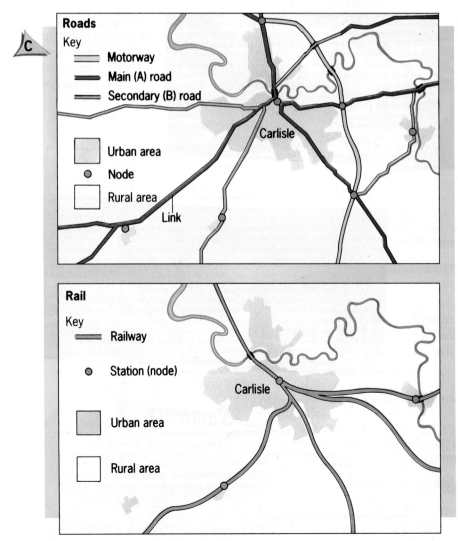

How can changes in transport networks affect people's lives?

By adding a new road (link) then the flow of traffic between two places (nodes) should be quicker and easier **but** ... as this is likely to increase the amount of traffic at the junction of the routes (node) then the result will be more congestion and pollution.

A **one-way system** allows traffic to flow more evenly and safely in one direction around the network **but** ... the new route will cause detours which will increase the distance of the journey.

When a new **bypass** (link) is built around a settlement (node) then one point (node) in the network will be eliminated making the journey for through traffic quicker and safer, and life in the settlement more peaceful **but** ... traders in the settlement will lose business (Activity 4). The closure of a railway line (link) or station (node) will make the rail network less dense **but** ... this will increase the number of people and vehicles on the road network.

One way

By-pass open
← A123

Anytown Station CLOSED

Activities

1 What is the difference between a link and a node?

2 Using the OS map (pages 82 and 83) and diagram **B**, compare the similarities and differences between the network density:
   a) of roads and railways
   b) in urban and rural areas.

3 Using an atlas compare:
   a) the main road network and the rail network for England and Wales

   b) the road network in an upland region like Wales or Scotland and a lowland region like south-east England.

4 Map **D** shows a new bypass. How has it affected the lives of the following groups of people?
   • the petrol station owner • children attending the village school • the farmer
   • residents of the housing estate • the shop and café owners • elderly residents
   • a long-distance lorry driver

D

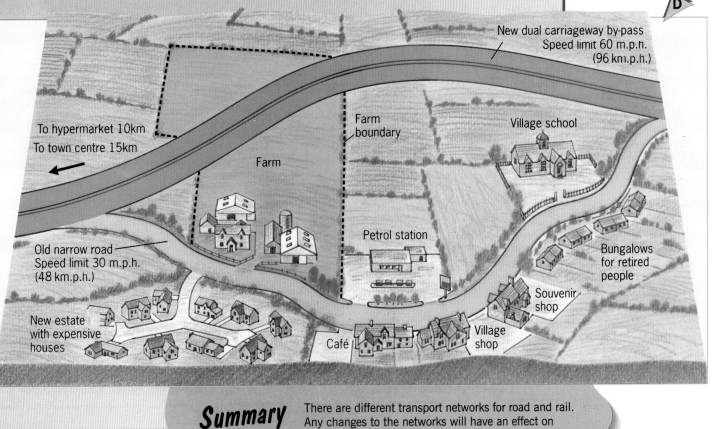

New dual carriageway by-pass
Speed limit 60 m.p.h.
(96 km.p.h.)

To hypermarket 10km
To town centre 15km

Farm boundary

Village school

Farm

Petrol station

Bungalows for retired people

Old narrow road
Speed limit 30 m.p.h.
(48 km.p.h.)

Souvenir shop

New estate with expensive houses

Café

Village shop

Summary

There are different transport networks for road and rail. Any changes to the networks will have an effect on people's lives.

▷ *Which is better – road or rail?* ◁

There are many different types of transport found across the world. Each type has its own advantages and disadvantages. Ideally a country needs several types of transport so that it can use the benefits of each. Britain has a wide choice, being an economically more developed country. Britain initially had the inventiveness and wealth to introduce new types of transport which have been continually modernised through new technological developments. Even so Britain is increasingly relying on just one type. By the mid-1990s over 90 per cent of passenger journeys and over 80 per cent of goods (freight) movements were by road (diagram **A**).

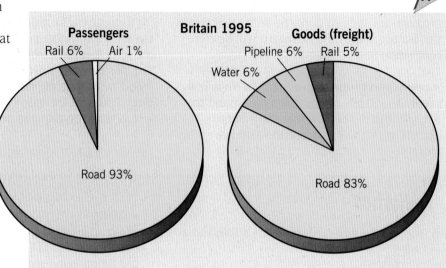

A

Britain 1995

Passengers
Rail 6%   Air 1%
Road 93%

Goods (freight)
Pipeline 6%   Rail 5%
Water 6%
Road 83%

B Advantages of road and rail

Road

Passengers
- Door-to-door convenience for work, shopping and leisure
- Can park outside or close to shops, friends' houses, work
- No timetable to keep to – greater flexibility
- Greater choice of routes (higher density)
- Cheaper for short journeys

Goods
- No 'break-of-bulk'. Once loaded, goods are not handled until arrival at their destination
- Quick delivery of light and perishable goods
- Vehicles specially designed for type of freight carried, e.g. refrigerated, air-conditioned
- Flexibility in timetable and choice of route

Rail

Passengers
- Comfortable and safe – passengers can read, sleep or work
- Routes link city centre to city centre
- No congestion during journey and no parking problems
- Causes far less pollution – trains are mainly diesel or electric
- Less affected by bad weather, e.g. fog, snow, ice
- Cheaper for longer journeys

Goods
- Good for heavy, bulky and non-perishable goods, e.g. coal, cement
- Can carry large volumes on each journey
- Safer for toxic and dangerous freight
- Fewer delays for route repairs

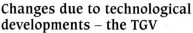
Changes due to technological developments – the TGV

The TGV (*Train à Grand Vitesse*) is the high-speed French train (photo **C**). It operates at average speeds of 270 km/hour (170 miles/hour) and is the fastest train in service in the world (the new trial German ICE train will take this record when it starts to carry passengers). When the first section was opened in 1983, travel times between Paris and Lyon were halved from four to two hours.

The high speeds and the good safety and punctuality records have been achieved through a series of technological developments. The TGV is computer-controlled and runs on new and specially designed track. This track has no level crossings and no tight curves. Slower trains carrying goods and local passengers run on adjacent updated lines.

Most French people are proud of their fast, safe and comfortable train. They appreciate its advanced technology and believe that the French rail system will become the centre of Europe's proposed high-speed network (map **D**). Parisian tourists can now reach the Mediterranean coast in three hours, and people living in towns near to the railway have benefited from an increase in the number of jobs available. But there is also growing opposition, especially from airlines and people living in the south-east of France. The government wish to build a second TGV link through Provence as the existing route to Nice is overcrowded. The proposed route would pass through several densely populated and forested areas and important vine growing districts. Local people believe that their environment has already been spoilt enough by 'tourists from the north'. Their protests, not always peaceful, have at times blocked roads and railways.

C French high-speed train – the TGV

D

Key
TGV routes — Existing
— Proposed
- - - National Boundaries

Map showing TGV routes in France including: Calais, Lille, Brussels, Rouen, Paris, Strasbourg, To Germany, Rennes, Dijon, Nantes, To Switzerland, Geneva, Limoges, Clermont Ferrand, Lyon, Turin, Grenoble, To Italy, Bordeaux, Nice, Montpellier, Marseille, Biarritz, Perpignan, To Spain. Also labelled: English Channel, Atlantic Ocean, Mediterranean Sea. Scale 0–100km, N compass.

Activities

1 a) What percentage of British passenger journeys are made by road?
   b) What percentage of British goods are sent by road?

2 a) Copy out table **E**. Complete it by listing three advantages of road transport and three advantages of rail transport.
   b) If both types of transport have advantages, why is road used far more than rail?

3 Your company's head office is in Brussels. You have to travel to a meeting in Nice.
   a) What is the shortest TGV route for the journey?
   b) Which towns will you go through?

4 How has the French TGV benefited from recent technological developments?

E

	Advantages: road	Advantages: rail
1		
2		
3		

Summary

Different forms of transport each have their own advantages and disadvantages. These can change as a result of technological and other developments.

▷ *How have transport developments affected economic activities?* ◁

Improvements to communications and changes in transport networks affect how people live. Transport and technological developments can affect a wide range of economic activities. The following examples illustrate some of these effects.

A
Information technology and where people work

Offices have always needed and used large amounts of information. In the past offices employed many typists and secretaries who often had to work in large rooms where information could easily be transferred. In turn these offices had to be near to other sources of information – libraries, commercial buildings such as banks, and other firms with whom they did business. Modern offices are now increasingly relying on **information technology (IT)** to transfer ideas and knowledge. The introduction of computers, word processors, fax machines and e-mail has reduced the number of employees needed, but has widened the choice of places where offices may locate and people can work. More people can work from home and send information by fax or on computer disc. Firms no longer have to locate in the expensive CBD (page 96), but can move to modern edge-of-city sites in

New office location at Shalford, Surrey

a more pleasant environment. Likewise, firms can move away from large urban areas to smaller towns in more rural parts of the country.

B **Bulk carriers and ports and port industries**

Left: Bulk carrier

Below: Sullum Voe oil terminal, Shetland

Before the 1960s thousands of dockers were needed to load and unload ships. It was hard, tiring, unreliable and badly paid work. Since then information technology has been used to reduce both labour costs and the time a ship spends in port. One change has been the building of huge bulk carriers. These carriers are specifically designed not just to carry large quantities but also to transport just one special cargo by sea, e.g. oil or iron ore.

To be successful a modern port has to have a large deepwater harbour capable of handling bulk carriers. Ships can reach ports located on the coast (e.g. Felixstowe) far more easily and quickly than ports situated up a river (e.g. London). New loading equipment has been introduced to handle specialist cargoes and large containers.

Whereas older ports had a range of industries, modern ones tend to specialise in one or two main industries based upon a limited range of imports. For example, Milford Haven has refineries using oil, and Port Talbot has steelworks using iron ore and coal. The surrounding environment may be put at risk from noise, fumes, spillage and explosions.

C Rapid air freight and market gardening

Air transport is usually better suited to carrying passengers than freight. However, certain goods can be carried if they are light in weight, are high in value and are **perishable**. Perishable goods include **market garden produce** such as fruit, vegetables and flowers. These have a short life and decay rapidly. If a market garden lies close to an airport, especially an international airport, then its goods can be sent quickly to other parts of the world.

Kenya, an economically developing country, needs to increase its exports to earn more money. Until recently limited amounts of fruit and vegetables were canned before being exported. Now an increasing number of farms with good road access to Nairobi Airport are growing fresh produce, such as pineapples and French beans, for export by air. A recent welcomed money-earner for Kenya is the export of freshly cut flowers, mainly carnations and orchids. Fast transit lorries to the airport mean the flowers can reach European markets within twelve hours. Unfortunately even large planes can only carry small amounts and at a high cost.

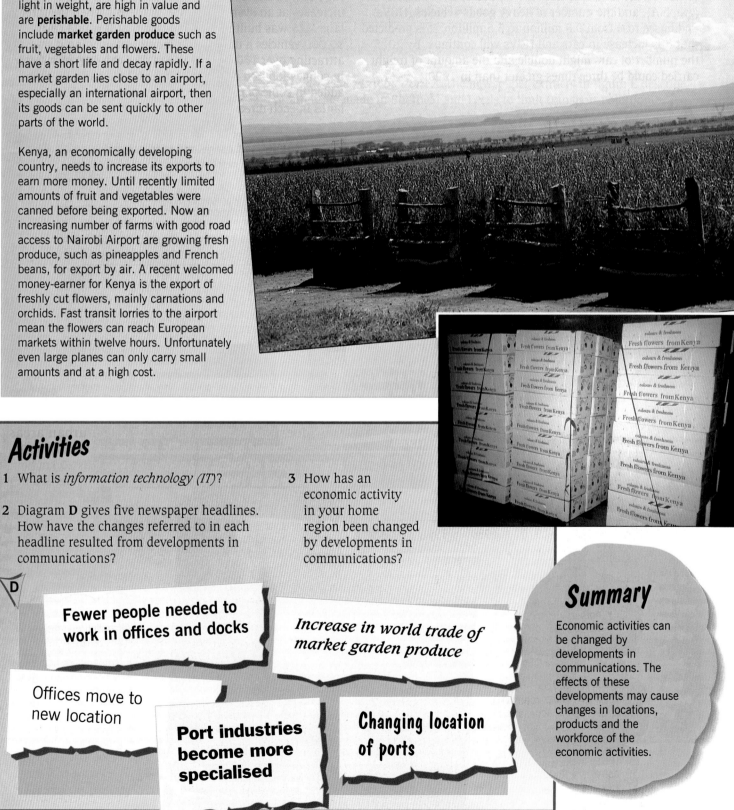

Carnations being grown in Kenya for export

Activities

1 What is *information technology (IT)*?

2 Diagram **D** gives five newspaper headlines. How have the changes referred to in each headline resulted from developments in communications?

3 How has an economic activity in your home region been changed by developments in communications?

D

Fewer people needed to work in offices and docks

Increase in world trade of market garden produce

Offices move to new location

Port industries become more specialised

Changing location of ports

Summary

Economic activities can be changed by developments in communications. The effects of these developments may cause changes in locations, products and the workforce of the economic activities.

How may urban traffic problems be reduced?

Environmental considerations are likely to be given a high priority in all future urban transport plans. People have become increasingly concerned about the effects of transport upon:

- human health (the increased incidence of asthma and breathing problems linked to vehicle emissions)
- the quality of their environment (noise, congestion, fumes)
- climatic change and global warming
- the economic cost of time wasted in traffic jams and in using a non-renewable source of energy.

Yet transport is not just an environmental issue. Future plans must allow all groups in the community to move around as safely, quickly and cheaply as possible. These plans must, however, be sustainable – they should improve people's mobility and safety without damaging the environment in which they live. Three such schemes at present in favour in the UK are described in fact files **A**, **B** and **C**.

Fact file A:
Manchester's Metrolink

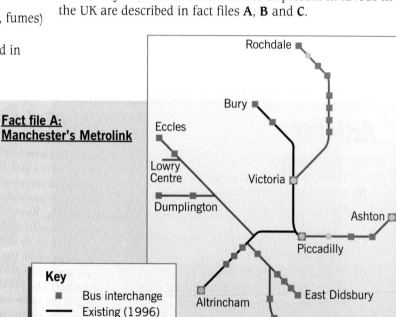

Key
- ■ Bus interchange
- ▬ Existing (1996)
- ▬ Proposed (2000)
- ● Rail interchange

First phase
(operating since 1992)
- ■ Britain's first purpose-built on-street light rail system linking Bury and Altrincham with the city centre (see map).
- ■ Conversion of two of the city's most heavily used suburban railways.
- ■ Construction of 3 km of new surface routes and four new stations in the city centre.
- ■ 26 stations, with those outside the CBD spaced, on average, 1.2 km apart.
- ■ Estimated 13 million passenger journeys (1996) – a saving of 2 million car journeys.

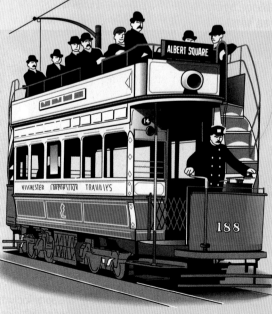

Source: National Tram Museum

An early 20th-century Manchester tram

'Supertrams' (see photo)
- ■ Maximum speed: 80 km/h on former railways, 50 km/h on roads.
- ■ Capacity: 206 (86 seated, 120 standing).
- ■ Timetable: 6 minutes during daytimes Monday to Saturday; 12–15 minutes at other times.
- ■ Electrically driven – reduces noise and air pollution, although pylons and overhead power cables create visual pollution.
- ■ for the estimated 20 per cent of users who are disabled/semi-disabled, and 20 per cent with pushchairs:
  - platforms at suburban stations at same level as tram-floor
  - retractable steps used at street-level and intermediate stations
  - narrowest possible gap between platforms and trams
  - spaces for wheelchairs and pushchairs near central doors
  - independently locking doors.
- ■ Automatic ticket machines at unmanned stations. Monitored by closed-circuit TV to catch fare-dodgers.

Fact file B: Park and ride schemes

Park and ride schemes:

■ allow private car owners living in rural areas to travel where public transport systems are unavailable or inadequate

■ provide free car parking, mainly at specially provided bus terminals, but sometimes at rail and metro stations, on the edge of urban areas

■ provide an efficient public transport system within urban areas

■ reduce the number of vehicles entering the city centre

■ reduce traffic fumes (air pollution), noise, congestion and land needed for car parking in the city centre

■ are mainly bus-based catering for commuters, shoppers and tourists working in or visiting the city centre

■ are usually bus services that operate non-stop to the city centre charging a fare comparable with the cost of city centre parking.

Park and ride

Fact file C: Traffic in residential areas

Problems

■ Increased volumes and speed of traffic:
  • creates safety problems for local residents
  • increases local air and noise pollution.

■ Large vehicles use residential areas to avoid congestion on main roads caused by the volumes of traffic or by temporary road works.

■ Parked cars limit the visibility of pedestrians.

■ Joy riding.

Solutions

■ Set up traffic calming schemes such as one-way streets, speed ramps, rumble strips and road narrowing.

■ Limit parking to local residents by issuing residents-only permits.

Activities

1 What is the difference between public transport and private transport?

2 List six problems created by traffic in urban areas.

3 a) Between which two places does the Manchester Metrolink ('supertram') operate?
   b) How does the Metrolink differ from traditional urban railways and existing bus services?
   c) How does the Metrolink improve:
      i) people's mobility and safety
      ii) the environment in which they live?
   d) What do you consider are its limitations?

4 Describe the advantages and disadvantages of:
   i) a park and ride scheme
   ii) one of the schemes shown in figure **D**.

5 a) Describe two traffic schemes, one in each of your local
   • town/city centre   • residential area.
   b) How successful do you think each scheme has been?

Meter
ZONE

Mon–Fri
8.30 am–6.30 pm
Saturday
8.30 am–1.30 pm

D

Summary

Traffic is a major problem in most urban areas. New plans aim to improve people's mobility and safety without further damaging the environment.

How can transport patterns be interpreted from OS maps?

Although atlas maps show physical features (relief and landforms) and human features (settlements and communications) of an area, these features can be shown in far greater detail and accuracy on Ordnance Survey (OS) maps. At times, however, OS maps show so much detail that it can be difficult to isolate and to identify patterns relating to just one of these topics. The OS map on pages 82 and 83 shows, amongst other detail, transport patterns in the Carlisle area. Map **A** has simplified the OS map by removing all detail not relevant in trying to recognise possible transport patterns.

Two reasons why Carlisle offered a good site for a settlement were:

1 several routes met here and
2 it was a good place to cross, or bridge, the river (page 85).

Carlisle is still a route centre with a **radial** transport network (map **B**). It is called radial because roads and railways radiate outwards, in all directions, like spokes in a bicycle wheel. Map **B** and the OS map show that the courses followed by these routes are determined by the relief of the land.

- They try to keep to low-lying land near to the coast.
- They take advantage of river valleys to pass through the many surrounding highland areas.
- They try to avoid being too close to rivers which may flood. This is especially true in Carlisle where the River Eden still floods most winters.

In mid-1993, The Department of Transport (DoT) announced their proposed route for a 9.4 km southern bypass of Carlisle. The aim would be to link the A595, the main road to West Cumbria, and the M6 (OS map, pages 82–83 and 115). At present traffic, including heavy lorries, has either to pass through the centre of Carlisle or travel along minor roads and through the villages of Dalston and Durdar. The DoT claim that a southern by-pass would 'remove through traffic from the city and the pleasant rural settlements and improve links between existing radial routes'.

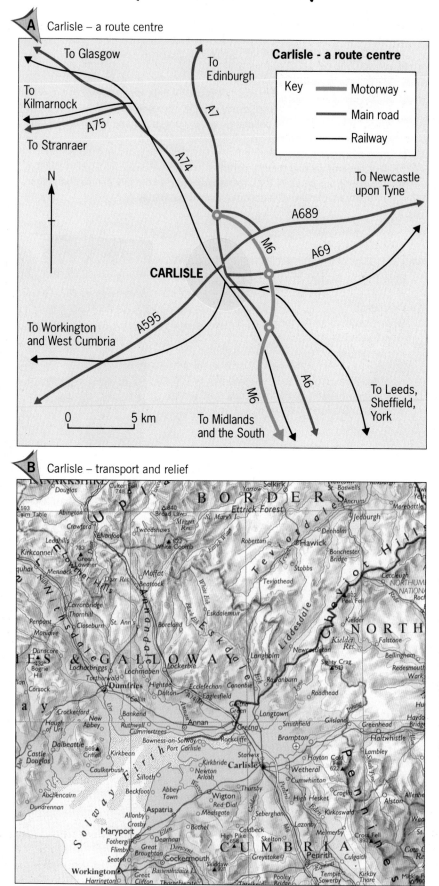

A Carlisle – a route centre

B Carlisle – transport and relief

Activities

1 Name the type of communication found at the following grid squares (pages 82 and 83).

a) 431570   e) 409567

b) 363527   f) 365565

c) 379571   g) 463535

d) 25525   h) 362542.

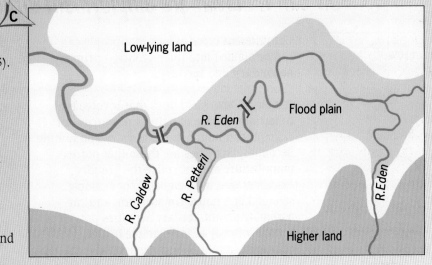

C

Low-lying land

Flood plain

R. Eden

R. Caldew

R. Petteril

R. Eden

Higher land

2 Map **C** shows the main relief features found on the OS map.

a) Make a copy of this map and add to it:
   i) the main roads and the M6
   ii) the railways.

b) Describe the routes taken by the roads and railways in relation to the main relief features.

c) Attempt the same two exercises using the OS map of your local area.

3 a) What do you think the traffic conditions were like in Carlisle before the M6 was built?

b) Using the OS map and map **B**, describe the course of the M6 in relation to:
   i) settlements
   ii) relief features.

4 Map **D** shows four routes considered by the DoT for a southern by-pass of Carlisle. They recommended route A/B. They rejected routes:

- C1/D/E1 and C2/D/E1 on environmental and economic grounds
- E1 because of damage to residential areas (property demolition, dividing a community, noise)
- C1/D/E2 and C2/D/E2 on environmental and economic grounds.

Using map evidence, suggest why the DoT:

a) recommended route AB

b) rejected each of the other three routes (i.e. effect on the environment; effect on residential areas; cost; etc.).

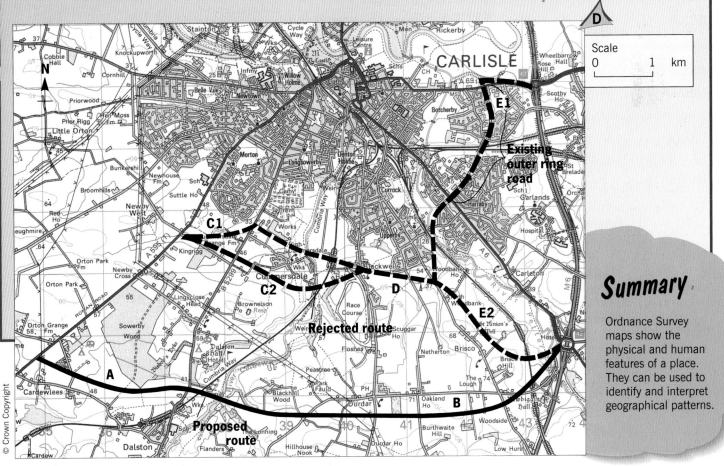

D

Scale
0   1   km

CARLISLE

Existing outer ring road

E1

E2

C1

C2

D

Rejected route

A

B

Proposed route

Summary

Ordnance Survey maps show the physical and human features of a place. They can be used to identify and interpret geographical patterns.

10 Employment structures

▷ What are employment structures? ◁

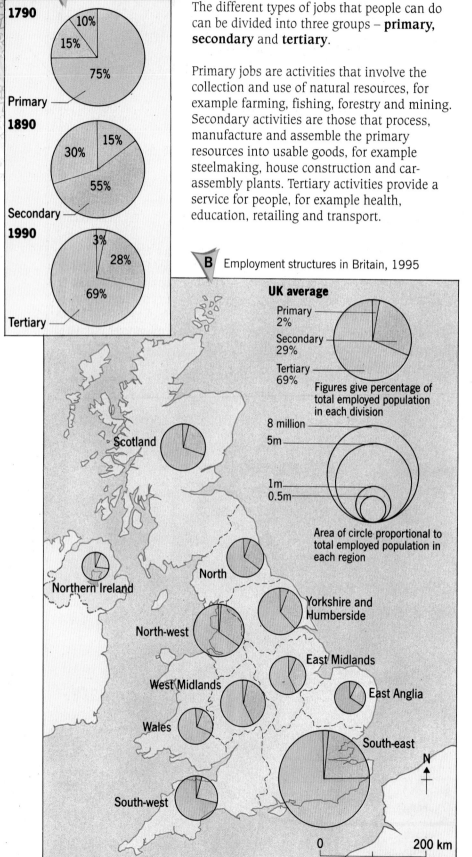

A

1790

10%
15%
75%
Primary —

1890

15%
30%
55%
Secondary —

1990

3%
28%
69%
Tertiary —

The different types of jobs that people can do can be divided into three groups – **primary, secondary** and **tertiary**.

Primary jobs are activities that involve the collection and use of natural resources, for example farming, fishing, forestry and mining. Secondary activities are those that process, manufacture and assemble the primary resources into usable goods, for example steelmaking, house construction and car-assembly plants. Tertiary activities provide a service for people, for example health, education, retailing and transport.

B Employment structures in Britain, 1995

UK average

Primary 2%
Secondary 29%
Tertiary 69%

Figures give percentage of total employed population in each division

8 million
5m
1m
0.5m

Area of circle proportional to total employed population in each region

Scotland

Northern Ireland

North

North-west

Yorkshire and Humberside

West Midlands

East Midlands

East Anglia

Wales

South-east

South-west

N

0   200 km

The proportion of people working in primary, secondary and tertiary activities in any place is called the **employment structure**. One method of illustrating the proportion of people employed in each group is by a pie graph (graph **A**). Employment structures can:

- change over a period of time (graph **A**)
- vary from place to place – i.e. between different towns or regions in Britain (map **B**) and between different countries (map **C**).

Change over time – the UK (graph A)

Before 1800 most people living in Britain earned a living from the land. The majority were farmers while many of the remainder made things either for use in farming (e.g. scythes) or from items produced by farmers (e.g. bread).

During the nineteenth century the main types of job changed dramatically, mainly as a result of the Industrial Revolution. Fewer people worked on the land and many moved to towns to find work. Many mined coal or worked in heavy industries making things like steel, ships and machinery.

Further changes have occurred in the twentieth century. Farming and industry have become more mechanised and need fewer workers. Coal and other natural resources are running out, while industry is faced with increasing competition from other countries. However, there are now many more hospitals, schools and shops. Transport has also provided numerous jobs.

All industrialised, developed countries have experienced these same changes.

Changes between places – within Britain

Map **B** shows employment structures in Britain. Every region has fewest workers in the primary sector and most in the tertiary. However, the proportion in each region varies considerably; for example, compare South-east England and the West Midlands. Also within each region there may be big differences between types of town. For example, one may be a market town, one an industrial centre and one a holiday resort.

Changes between countries

Map **C** shows the employment structures for 16 countries which are at different stages of economic development. It also divides the world into two economic parts. Countries to the north and east of the dividing line are the 'rich' countries and those to the south and west are the 'poor' countries. (See if you can suggest exceptions to this statement.)

- In most of the rich, or economically more developed, countries there are relatively few people employed in the primary sector, a higher proportion in the secondary sector and most in the tertiary sector.
- By contrast in the poorer, or economically less developed, countries most people find jobs in the primary sector, and relatively few are employed in the secondary and tertiary sectors. Usually it is the primary jobs that are the most poorly paid.

C World employment structures

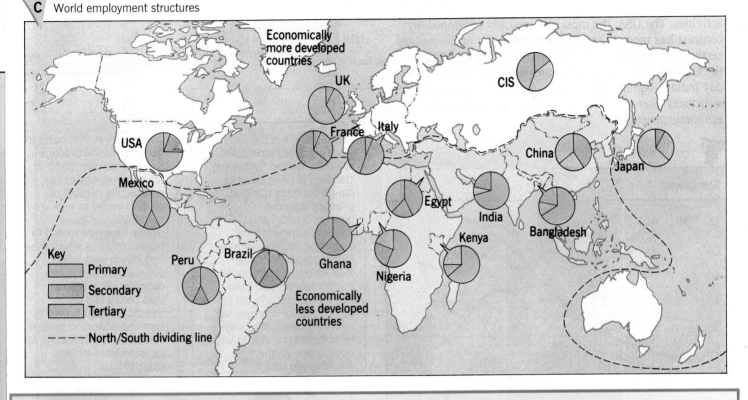

Activities

1 In your own words give the definitions for primary, secondary and tertiary activities, and employment structures.

2 a) List the following jobs under the three headings of **Primary**, **Secondary** and **Tertiary**:
   - teacher • doctor • police officer • bus driver • farmer
   - bricklayer • steelworker • nurse • shopkeeper • pop singer • ambulance driver • bank manager • plumber
   - quarry worker • forestry worker • shop assistant.

   b) Copy and complete table **D**.

3 a) Using map **C** list those countries with over:
   i) 50 per cent employed in the primary sector
   ii) 50 per cent employed in the tertiary sector.

   b) Describe the
   i) location of economic development
   ii) level of economic development of the countries which you named in part **a)**.

   c) Is graph **E** for a developed or a developing country? Give three reasons for your answer.

D

Primary	Secondary	Tertiary
Lumberjack	Sawmill operator	Furniture shop assistant
Dairy farmer		
North Sea oil rig worker		
	Bricklayer	
		Car sales person

E

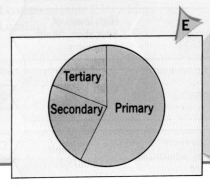

Summary

The proportion of people employed in primary, secondary and tertiary activities changes over time and differs between countries.

Why is agricultural land use changing?

Despite the efforts of Mr Hitchen and other dairy farmers to produce more milk, Britain is still not self-sufficient in dairy produce. However, Britain is no longer in isolation but is part of the European Union. One outcome is that British farmers are subject to decisions made under the EU's **Common Agricultural Policy (CAP)**. There are several other areas within the EU which are very important for dairy farming, notably Denmark and the Netherlands. Taken as a group, EU farmers, including dairy farmers, overproduced certain commodities. This created the so-called 'mountains and lakes' surpluses (diagram **A**), which included milk and butter. The surplus products were stored, at a high cost, as they were not needed by EU countries. Nor could they be sold to the many countries with food shortages because they were too poor to be able to buy the produce or because of existing trade restrictions. The EU came under increasing pressure to try to reduce its farm surpluses. It is claimed that 70 per cent of the EU's money went on helping farmers to produce food which often was not needed, while agriculture, in return, only provided about 5 per cent of the total income of the EU.

How do changing EU farm policies affect dairying?
The EU has made major changes to the CAP in an attempt to reduce its 'mountains and lakes' and the money that it spends on agriculture.

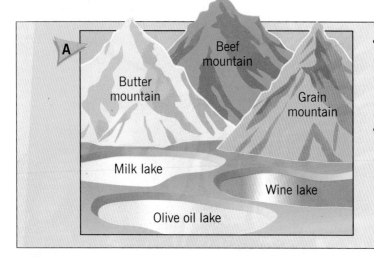

A
Butter mountain
Beef mountain
Grain mountain
Milk lake
Wine lake
Olive oil lake

- Dairy farmers can no longer produce as much milk as they wish but are given a **quota** which they must not exceed. They still receive the subsidy for their quota but they can be fined if they try to exceed it. The quota is for less milk than was previously produced.

- Dairy farmers are encouraged to **'set-aside'** part of their farm and are paid if they do **not** produce food on up to 15 per cent of their land. The payment is made on the understanding that the land will not be used for food production for a minimum of five years. Farmers have the option of leaving it fallow or using it for non-agricultural purposes (table **D**).

B Kilnsey Park Trout Farm, Yorkshire

What are the options available to Mr Hitchen?
Mr Hitchen's quota means that he has had to reduce his herd from 160 cows (page 123) to 100. Even with the guaranteed subsidy his income is no longer enough for his farm to remain profitable. If he is to continue farming, which he wants to do, then he is going to have to make changes. He has several options. These are summarised in diagram **D**.

C

Farmland converted into a wetland wildlife site

Economically less develo
especially those in sub-Sa
have any fossil fuels of th
less likely to have the we
requirements. Several did
they have been unable to
prestigious hydro-electric
non-industrialised count
have to rely upon fuelwo
source of energy.

Fuelwood can account fo
the energy consumed by

C

Bangladesh 0.08	
Kenya 0.11	
Ghana 0.14	Eco
Nigeria 0.21	less
India 0.35	cou
Egypt 0.70	
Brazil 0.81	
Russ	

0   2

D

	SCHEME		ADVANTAGES	DISADVANTAGES
1 Within farming	a) Diversify farming		Grow some cereals, e.g. barley. Less reliance on milk quotas.	Cereals not suited to the climate of Cheshire.
	b) Improve milk quality		Higher-quality milk receives higher subsidies (i.e. fewer bacteria to treat).	There is a limit to improvement and increase in subsidy.
	c) Increase quota		Done by buying a neighbouring farm and using its quota.	Very expensive to buy another farm. Puts another farmer out of business. Will EU reduce quotas again?
2 Set-aside	d) Leave fallow (under grass)		Most popular option with farmers. Costs no money. Receives a payment – about £200 a hectare. Land use not changed.	No big improvement in income, possibly only a short-term solution.
3 Alter land use	e) Woodland		Management scheme. Given grants for up to £190 per hectare to plant trees. Higher grants for deciduous trees than for conifers.	Slow growing. No income for many years.
	f) Wildlife scheme		Re-creation of a pond/wetland site. Re-planting hedgerows. Small grants from conservation agencies.	No real income even though it would improve the environment.
	g) Recreation		E.g. Golf course, trout farm, scrambling, riding, stables, camp site, education visits. Widens chance of income.	Often involves a lot of initial investment which farmer is unlikely to have. Some threaten the natural environment.

Activities

1 a) What is meant by
     i)   Renewable res
     ii) Non-renewabl
     iii) Fossil fuels
   b) What are the follo
        • nuclear
        • solar
        • tidal
        • biogas

2 The three graphs in **I**
   energy for Kenya, th
   necessarily in that o
   a) name which cour
   b) give two reasons
   c) draw a graph to
        in energy sources
   d) give reasons for
        have shown in p

Activities

1 a) What is the Common Agricultural Policy?
   b) Why is there a surplus of dairy produce in the EU?
   c) There should be five newspaper headlines in diagram **E**, but each has been torn into two.
      i)   Match up the ten torn pieces to give the five original correct headlines.
      ii) Explain how two of these headlines refer to attempts by the EU to reduce its 'milk lake' and 'butter mountain'.
      iii) How do the remaining headlines suggest other ways by which the EU could reduce its surplus even further?

2 Mr Hitchen is going to have to find an extra source of income. This will probably mean changing the land use of part of his farm. A change in land use will also affect the environment. Look at the schemes in diagram **D**.
   a) Which do you think is his most attractive option
      i)   economically
      ii) environmentally?
   b) Which do you think is his least attractive option
      i)   economically
      ii) environmentally?

E

EU produces food at high cost

Poorer communities cannot afford the price of food produced by the EU

Farmers to be paid to take land out of production

Food surplus in EU

Less milk will be produced

Trade agreement stops EU food going to developing countries

EU introduces set-aside land scheme

EU to cut quotas

Famine in Africa gets worse

African countries have little money to buy food

Summary

By subsidising farmers the EU has built up a large food surplus in several products. As the EU changes its policies to reduce the surplus, it means some farmers are having to change the land use on their farms or go out of business.

▷ *Why do some industries group together?* ◁

When looking at a simple urban land use model (diagram **A**, page 94), it can be seen that certain types of economic activity group together. Shops and offices group together in the CBD. Older nineteenth-century industries located in today's inner city areas. Firms wishing to locate on modern industrial estates or on science parks group together on the outskirts of urban areas. There have always been advantages for similar types of firms and industries to group together in particular locations (diagram **A**).

A

Old inner city area

CBD

Nineteenth-century terraced housing and industry

Inter-war, medium cost housing

Modern housing estates, industrial estates, business and science parks

Edge of city

Rural area with commuter villages

Concentration of shops and offices (page 144).

Inner city
Concentration of industries, many of which developed in the nineteenth century. The area may still include old mills and factories, or it may have been redeveloped with smaller units and DIY stores.

Advantages of inner cities:
* near commercial centre (CBD)
* near main roads leading into city centre
* next to railways and canals
* near to workforce living in low-cost, terraced housing
* at time of development this location was on the edge of the urban area
* small firms making component parts for larger, nearby assembly companies

Edge of city
Concentration of modern firms on industrial estates and science parks.

Advantages of edge-of-city locations:
* cheaper sites as land values decrease away from the CBD
* need large areas of land for car parking and possible future expansion
* near to main roads and motorway interchanges
* near skilled and mainly female workforce in modern private housing estates and commuter villages
* easier to exchange information with similar types of firm
* attractive layout (diagram **B**) with 70 per cent of science parks left as open space

A

Non-renewable r

These resources

75% of energy c
fossil fuels. They
'fossil' because t
remains of plant

Coal, fuelwood,
natural gas

89% world's en

Relatively cheap
only be used on
destruction to th

RENE

Nucl
5%

Fuelwood

Natu

Science and business parks

Both **science** and **business parks** are located on edge-of-city greenfield sites. They have attractive layouts (figures **B** and **C**) with grassy areas, ornamental gardens and ponds, and buildings screened by trees. The modern buildings have central heating, air conditioning and large windows allowing in the maximum amount of light. Each unit has plenty of space for car parking. Many of the firms are connected with the information, **high-technology**, and electronics industries. Whereas science parks have direct links with universities for research, business parks may also include superstores, hotels and leisure centres.

What are the disadvantages of similar firms concentrating together?

If all firms in a given area require the same levels of skill, some may find difficulty in recruiting the right type of workforce. It is possible that too many similar industries might produce too many goods for people in the local area to buy. If a town relies too much on a particular type of industry it is more likely to experience unemployment if that industry is hit by a recession.

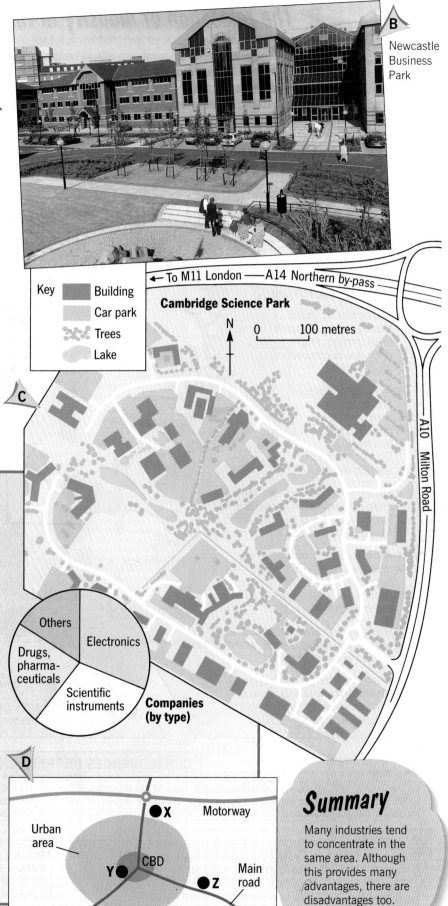

B Newcastle Business Park

Key
- Building
- Car park
- Trees
- Lake

← To M11 London ── A14 Northern by-pass →

Cambridge Science Park

N   0   100 metres

A10 Milton Road

C

D

Companies (by type)
- Others
- Electronics
- Drugs, pharmaceuticals
- Scientific instruments

Motorway
X
Urban area
CBD
Y
Z
Main road

Activities

1 Figure **C** shows the layout of Cambridge Science Park.
   a) What is a science park?
   b) Name three types of company found on the Cambridge Science Park.
   c) What are the advantages of locating on this particular site?
   d) What are the advantages to the companies of concentrating together on the same site?
   e) What are the disadvantages to the companies of concentrating together on the same site?
   f) Describe the layout of the Cambridge Science Park under these headings.
   - Buildings
   - Road pattern
   - Landscaped areas

2 Diagram **D** shows three possible locations for a new science park.
   a) Which of the three locations would you choose? Give reasons for your choice.
   b) Why would you reject the other two sites?

Summary

Many industries tend to concentrate in the same area. Although this provides many advantages, there are disadvantages too.

▷ *What affects the economic development*

One important factor affecting the economic growth of a country is the nature of, and the value placed upon, natural resources. Often natural resources, such as mineral wealth or the potential to produce high-yielding foods, are limited. When resources, especially minerals, are available, economically developing countries often lack the capital and the technology to develop them. As a result most of the available resources are bought, at as low a price as possible, by the richer and already industrialised economically more developed countries. Having traded their natural resources at a low price, developing countries have then to buy back these materials in a processed (manufactured) form at a much higher price. The resultant trade deficit means even less money is available to try to develop their own resources.

A

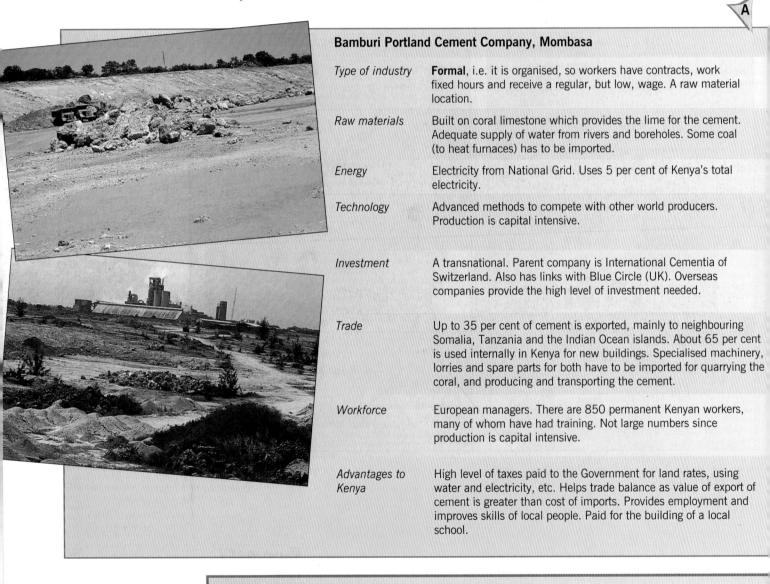

Bamburi Portland Cement Company, Mombasa

Type of industry	**Formal**, i.e. it is organised, so workers have contracts, work fixed hours and receive a regular, but low, wage. A raw material location.
Raw materials	Built on coral limestone which provides the lime for the cement. Adequate supply of water from rivers and boreholes. Some coal (to heat furnaces) has to be imported.
Energy	Electricity from National Grid. Uses 5 per cent of Kenya's total electricity.
Technology	Advanced methods to compete with other world producers. Production is capital intensive.
Investment	A transnational. Parent company is International Cementia of Switzerland. Also has links with Blue Circle (UK). Overseas companies provide the high level of investment needed.
Trade	Up to 35 per cent of cement is exported, mainly to neighbouring Somalia, Tanzania and the Indian Ocean islands. About 65 per cent is used internally in Kenya for new buildings. Specialised machinery, lorries and spare parts for both have to be imported for quarrying the coral, and producing and transporting the cement.
Workforce	European managers. There are 850 permanent Kenyan workers, many of whom have had training. Not large numbers since production is capital intensive.
Advantages to Kenya	High level of taxes paid to the Government for land rates, using water and electricity, etc. Helps trade balance as value of export of cement is greater than cost of imports. Provides employment and improves skills of local people. Paid for the building of a local school.

Activity

The Bamburi Portland Cement Company is a formal industry developed by a transnational company. Jua Kali are groups of informal industries which have grown spontaneously.

a) What is the difference between a formal and an informal industry?

b) What effect do the development of industries like the Bamburi Portland Cement Company and small-scale Jua Kali enterprises have on the economic development of an economically

# of an economically developing country?

Industrial development is also affected by the amounts and type of inward investment from the government within a country, or through foreign investment, loans and development assistance programmes. These, and other factors, may provide opportunities for the economic development of a country, but more often put constraints upon it.

Two extreme examples, taken from Kenya, have been selected to try to show how the factors listed earlier can affect economic growth. They are the large Bamburi Portland Cement Company near Mombasa (figure **A**) and the Jua Kali metal workshops in Nairobi (figure **B**).

B

Jua Kali metal workshops, Nairobi

Type of industry	**Informal**, i.e. spontaneous jobs, often small-scale family enterprises. Long and irregular hours, low and uncertain wages. A market location.
Raw materials	Cheap scrap metal is recycled by melting it down and hammering it into various shapes, e.g. locks, boxes, cooking utensils, water barrels. Charcoal is used to heat the scrap metal.
Energy	Manual labour.
Technology	Appropriate technology which is sustainable and suited to the skills of the people, the availability of raw materials and capital. Labour intensive.
Investment	Very limited. The Government (inward investment) has supported this Jua Kali scheme by providing roofs to protect the workers from the weather (Jua Kali means 'under the hot sun'). There are many types of Jua Kali in Nairobi.
Trade	All the products are sold and used locally.
Workforce	Over 1000 workers in an area about 300 m x 100 m. Workers have had to develop their own skills. Large numbers since production is labour intensive.
Advantages to Kenya	Estimates suggest 600 000 people are employed in 350 000 small-scale Jua Kali enterprises in Kenya. Enterprising spirit. Firms need little capital, recycle materials which otherwise would be wasted, provide low-cost training, and can react quickly to market changes. They provide the backbone for Kenya's industrial development.

developing country like Kenya? Give your answer under the following headings.
- Use of natural resources
- Technology
- Trade
- Inward (internal) investment
- Foreign investment

Summary

Several factors including the nature and value of natural resources, the level and development of technology, the balance of trade, the amount and type of inward investment, and the significance of foreign investments, can all affect the economic growth of economically developing countries.

13 Tertiary (service) activities

Shopping in British towns in the 1960s and 1970s

The concept of a **shopping hierarchy**, ranging from large regional shopping centres down to the village or corner shop, has already been described (page 89). During the 1960s and 1970s, four main types of shop and shopping centre could be identified in British towns and cities. Diagram **A** shows how the four types fit into an urban hierarchy. Diagram **B** shows, by means of a simplified transect, their generalised location.

A

CBD	**High order centre** (usually only one) Sells: comparison, luxury and specialist goods
Secondary centres and suburban parades	**Middle order centres** (usually several) Sell: a mixture of convenience and specialist goods
Corner shops	**Low order centres** (many) Sell: convenience goods

C

D

The city centre (CBD)

- Commercial and shopping centre. Accessible as most main roads meet here.
- Area of largest number of shops, biggest shops, and most shoppers.
- Large department stores and superstores which can afford the high land values.
- Comparison shops (e.g. clothes, shoes) where style and prices can be compared.
- Specialist shops (e.g. jewellery, furniture, electrical goods).
- Small food shops (e.g. bakers, grocers, butchers and fishmongers).
- Some out-of-door pedestrian precincts, but most streets shared between cars, buses, delivery lorries and shoppers.

Secondary shopping centres

- Usually a line of shops extending alongside main roads leading into the city centre.
- Take advantage of cheaper land values, easier parking facilities, passing traffic and good accessibility.
- Many shops rely on impulse buying.
- Includes car showrooms and petrol stations.
- Some specialist shops (e.g. florists, food take-aways, off-licences).
- Some convenience shops (e.g. newsagents).

Activities

1 What is the difference between:
   a) low order and high order goods
   b) convenience and specialist goods?

2 Look at diagram **B**. Which part of the shopping transect does your local area fall into? Draw a plan of your local area and label the types of shops in it.

3 How have a) accessibility and b) land values affected the type of shops found in:
   i)   the city centre (CBD)
   ii) a secondary shopping centre
   iii) an inner city housing area
   iv) a suburban parade?

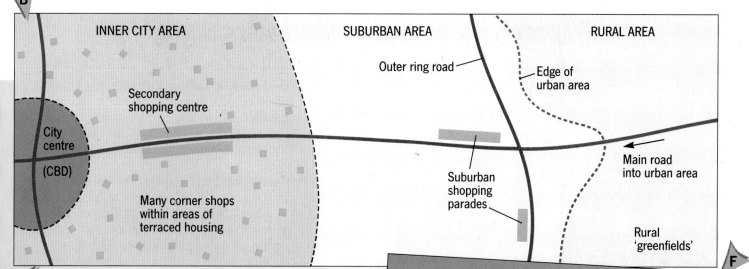

INNER CITY AREA

SUBURBAN AREA

RURAL AREA

Secondary
shopping centre

Outer ring road

Edge of
urban area

City
centre
(CBD)

Main road
into urban area

Many corner shops
within areas of
terraced housing

Suburban
shopping
parades

Rural
'greenfields'

Corner shops

- Date from the nineteenth century and before the time of cars and public transport. Had to be easily accessible as people had to walk to them.
- Sell convenience goods – items people need daily but are not necessarily prepared to travel long distances to buy (e.g. milk, bread, newspapers, sweets).
- Open long and irregular hours for local people who might work late, receive unexpected guests or who have forgotten odd items.
- Friendly atmosphere. Social meeting place especially for elderly people living alone.

Suburban shopping parades

- Found in the suburbs either alongside main roads leading into the city centre or within large, modern housing estates. In both cases they provide easy access for local people.
- Save people who live near the edge of the urban area from having to travel into the city centre.
- Usually have limited space for car parking.
- Mainly convenience shops and small chain stores (e.g. Spar, VG).
- A few specialist shops (e.g. chemist, baker, post office).

Summary

Different types of shopping centres can be placed into a hierarchy based upon their size and the services that they provide. It is possible to identify a pattern showing the distribution of these various shopping centres within an urban area. This pattern is affected by accessibility, land values and the sequence of urban development.

Why have shopping habits and patterns changed?

Today's shoppers are more discerning in their choice of goods and the places where they shop. They are increasingly better educated and more aware through travel and television, and require sophistication and convenience in the shopping environment. Increased car ownership, more working women and greater demands on leisure time have resulted in less frequent food shopping. Bulk buying and late night shopping are now commonplace.

Source: GeoActive, Spring 1993, 'Recent Trends in Retailing in the UK'

Increased mobility Due to the increase in car ownership, and two-car families, people can travel further to shops, visit shops with a wider range and volume of stock, and buy in bulk.

Accessibility Improved urban roads and national motorways enable shoppers, and delivery lorries, to travel more easily and more quickly to new shopping centres. Many of these new centres have an edge-of-city location.

Bulk buying Many shoppers now buy in bulk either once a week or once a month. This is a result of more people being paid monthly, having less free time, owning a deep-freezer, and being able to park their cars near to the shop exit. Bulk buying is also cheaper.

Space Many new superstores and hypermarkets have been built on edge-of-city locations (pages 147 to 149). They need large areas of space for their buildings, car parks and quality environment, land that is relatively cheap to buy, room for expansion and good access by road.

Population movement The location of shops has altered as an increasing number of people move out of urban areas, especially the inner city and conurbations, into suburban areas and smaller rural towns.

Shopping hours Partly due to the increasing number of women in paid employment, a greater number of shops open later on many evenings and, more recently, on Sundays.

Left: Queensgate Shopping Centre, Peterborough
Below: Union Street, Bath

A

Changes in the CBD

- An increase in both pedestrianised precincts and covered shopping centres. Covered shopping malls shield shoppers from the weather and shorten the distances between shops.
- An increase in the number of food supermarkets which has resulted in the closure of specialist shops such as butchers, fishmongers and small grocers.
- Many large furniture and carpet stores moved out of the city centre.
- The spaces created were filled by building societies, estate agents, small restaurants and cafés, and even more clothes shops.

B

Changes in the inner city

- Many corner shops have been pulled down during redevelopment schemes.
- Others have closed either because their goods were too expensive and limited in choice compared with city centre supermarkets, or because of people moving out of the area.
- Some corner shops now specialise in ethnic foods.
- DIY, furniture and carpet discount warehouses have opened along main roads leading into the city centre or on sites previously occupied by factories and terraced housing.

C

Changes on the edges of urban areas

- Major developments on cheaper, unused land in an edge-of-city, greenfield location.
- Developments include superstores (over 2500 m² of selling space, car parking and quality environment), hypermarkets (over 4500 m²), regional shopping centres (over 45 000 m²) and retail parks (pages 148 and 149).
- Smaller developments may only have food-halls. Larger ones are likely to contain DIY and garden centres, furniture and car salesrooms, and leisure facilities.

Activities

1 Photographs **D**, **E** and **F** (pages 144–145) and **A**, **B** and **C** (pages 146–147) all show different types of shop. Similar types of shop are found in most urban areas in Britain. Copy out and complete table **D** by answering **a)** and **b)**.

   a) Match up the following map references, taken from the OS map of Carlisle on pages 82 and 83, with the type of shop that might be found there.
   - 401559 • 408551 • 398554 • 393559
   - 393596 • 422545

   b) Name a place in your home or nearest urban area where that type of shop might be found.

   c) Give reasons for your answers to part **b)**.

2 With reference to changes in shopping patterns in your nearest urban area:

   a) Are most shops still found in the city centre?

D

Shopping centre	OS reference on Carlisle map	Example from your nearest urban area
Secondary shopping centre		
Corner shop		
Suburban parade		
City centre (CBD)		
New redevelopment in inner city		
Edge-of-city hypermarket		

b) Are the largest shops still found in the city centre?

c) Do most people still shop in the city centre?

d) What changes have taken place in the city centre in the last two years?

e) What changes have taken place in the inner city areas?

f) Has much edge-of-city shopping development taken place?

Summary

Factors such as the mobility of shoppers, the accessibility of shopping areas, bulk buying, the need for more space, and urban development schemes have all affected the pattern showing the location of shopping centres in British towns and cities.

▶ *Why have large shopping centres developed on the edges of cities?* ◀

The most important change in retailing in Britain since 1980 has been the rapid growth of edge-of-city shopping centres. It has been estimated that during this time four-fifths of all new shopping floor-space has been on out-of-town sites. Hypermarkets were the first to react to people's changing shopping habits (page 146). More recently, larger regional shopping centres have developed, based on the MetroCentre in Gateshead. Since then three other centres have opened (map **A**), including that at Meadowhall in Sheffield (photo **B** and plan **D**).

A UK regional shopping centres

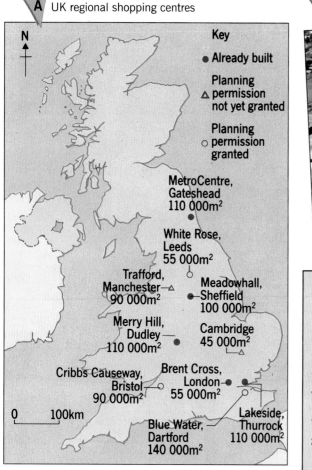

Key
● Already built
△ Planning permission not yet granted
○ Planning permission granted

MetroCentre, Gateshead 110 000m²
White Rose, Leeds 55 000m²
Trafford, Manchester 90 000m²
Meadowhall, Sheffield 100 000m²
Merry Hill, Dudley 110 000m²
Cambridge 45 000m²
Cribbs Causeway, Bristol 90 000m²
Brent Cross, London 55 000m²
Blue Water, Dartford 140 000m²
Lakeside, Thurrock 110 000m²

0   100km

B Meadowhall shopping centre

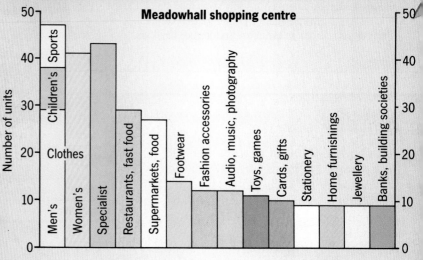

Meadowhall shopping centre

(Number of units)

Clothes: Men's, Women's, Specialist
Children's, Sports
Restaurants, fast food
Supermarkets, food
Footwear
Fashion accessories
Audio, music, photography
Toys, games
Cards, gifts
Stationery
Home furnishings
Jewellery
Banks, building societies

Advantages of an edge-of-city location
• They are near main roads and, ideally, a motorway interchange which makes the delivery of goods easier and gives access to shoppers from several large urban areas. Allows closer links with retailers selling similar goods.
• There is plenty of space for large car parks as hypermarkets and regional centres aim to attract motorists (over 12 000 parking places at the MetroCentre). No parking problems or traffic congestion as there is in the city centre.
• Land values are lower than those in the CBD, and so too are the rates and rent which shop-owners have to pay. This allows individual shops to use large areas of floor-space and to keep the prices of their goods down. Being so large, shops can stock a large volume and a wide range of goods.
• Unlike the city centre, there is plenty of space for possible future expansion.
• They are near to suburban housing estates which provide a workforce, especially as many employees are female, work part-time, and have to work late most evenings.

The majority of shoppers are relatively young, are car owners, are prepared to travel considerable distances, buy in bulk, and shop relatively infrequently.

The larger regional centre developments provide a wide range of associated facilities such as petrol stations, restaurants and leisure facilities. Sir John Hall, who pioneered this type of shopping at the MetroCentre, has said: 'The emphasis has to be laid on family shopping and associated leisure activities. In other words, it is to provide a day out for the whole family.' Plan **D** shows the layout for the lower of the two shopping malls in Sheffield's Meadowhall Centre, and graph **C** the number and types of shops and amenities available in the centre.

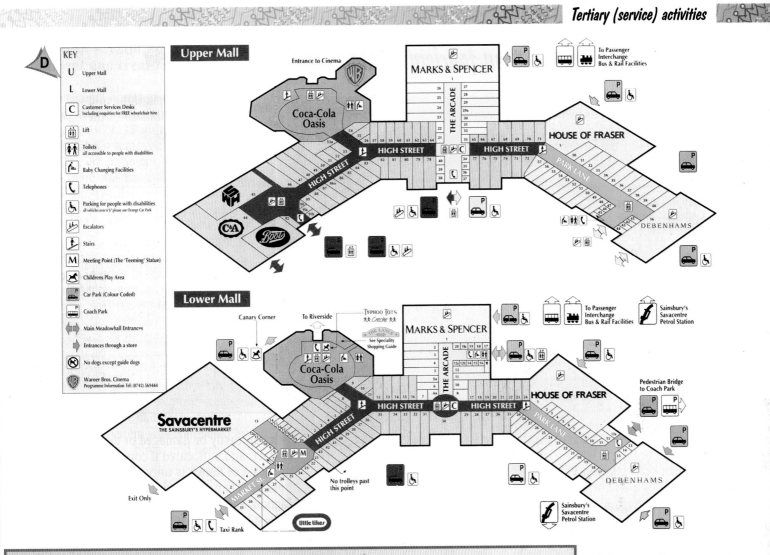

KEY

U Upper Mall

L Lower Mall

C Customer Services Desks
Including enquiries for FREE wheelchair hire

Lift

Toilets
all accessible to people with disabilities

Baby Changing Facilities

Telephones

Parking for people with disabilities
all vehicles over 6'6" please use Orange Car Park

Escalators

Stairs

M Meeting Point (The 'Teeming' Statue)

Childrens Play Area

Car Park (Colour Coded)

Coach Park

Main Meadowhall Entrances

Entrances through a store

No dogs except guide dogs

Warner Bros. Cinema
Programme Information Tel: (0742) 569444

Lower Mall

Activities

1 A large national supermarket chain wishes to build a hypermarket in the area shown on map **E**. Five available sites have been shown as **J** to **N**. Some sites will not be acceptable to the supermarket chain, other sites will not be acceptable to local people and the planners.

a) Rank the five sites in the order which you think that the supermarket chain will prefer. Give reasons for your answer.

b) Which of the sites do you think will:
   i) cause most opposition from local people
   ii) be rejected by the planners?
   Give reasons for your answer.

c) On which site do you think the hypermarket will eventually be built?

2 a) Give five advantages of building a regional shopping centre at Meadowhall, on the edge of Sheffield.

b) According to graph **C**, what are the three major users of the units in the centre?

c) Why is the centre a good place:
   i) for family shopping
   ii) for a day out for the whole family?

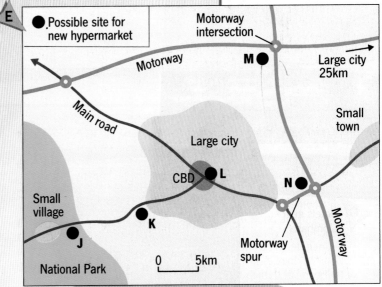

Summary

As city centres have become more crowded and expensive, and as people's mobility and shopping preferences change, a large number of new shops have chosen an edge-of-city location.

149

How can conflicting demands arise in National Parks?

A

Key
- National Parks
- Other areas with National Park status

N

Northumberland (moors, forests)

Newcastle upon Tyne

Yorkshire Dales (moors, valleys, limestone)

Lake District (lakes, mountains, coasts)

Leeds

North York Moors (moors, coast)

Liverpool

Sheffield

Snowdonia (mountains, lakes, coast)

Manchester

Peak District (moors, valleys, limestone, millstone grit)

Birmingham

Pembrokeshire Coast (coast)

Norfolk Broads (wetlands)

Brecon Beacons (moors, limestone)

Cardiff   Bristol

London

Exmoor (moors, coast)

Exeter

New Forest (woodland)

Dartmoor (moors, tors, valleys)

0   100 km

Ten National Parks in England and Wales were set up by an Act of Parliament in 1949. The National Parks, which cover nearly 10 per cent of the two countries, were chosen because of their great natural beauty and scenic attraction (map **A**). They contain some of the most diverse upland and/or coastal scenery in England and Wales. The Act also created National Park Authorities whose task it was to look after the Parks. Each National Park Authority has to:
- protect and enhance the landscape
- help the public to relax, and encourage them to participate in outdoor recreational activities.

To these can be added another duty:
- to protect the social and economic well-being of people who live and/or work in the National Park.

The term 'National Park' can be misleading. They are not 'parks' in the sense of an urban park. The public do not have complete freedom to wander where they would like. Unlike most National Parks in Europe and America, they are not 'national' in the sense that they are owned by the nation. They are though considered to be 'national' because their beauty and leisure opportunities are vital to the country. These two misconceptions can lead to conflicts between different land owners and different land users. Figure **B** shows who owns the land in the National Parks.

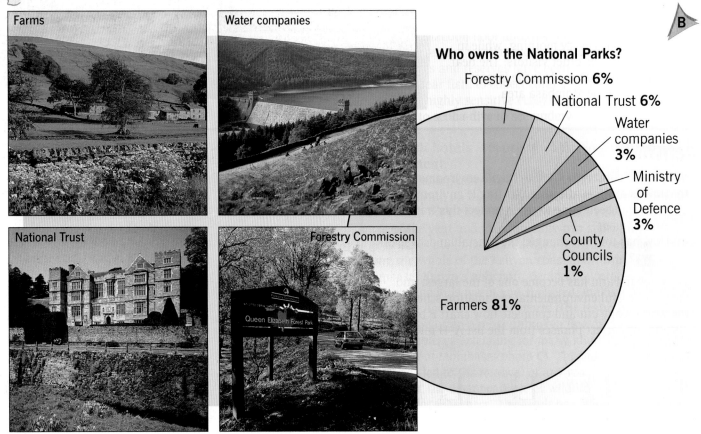

B

Farms

Water companies

National Trust

Forestry Commission

Queen Elizabeth Forest Park

Who owns the National Parks?

Forestry Commission **6%**

National Trust **6%**

Water companies **3%**

Ministry of Defence **3%**

County Councils **1%**

Farmers **81%**

How can conflicts occur?

Between different land users Farmers may want more land; the Forestry Commission may want to plant more trees; water companies may want to build another reservoir; the Ministry of Defence want to keep people off their land; property developers want to build holiday homes; tourists want to have free access to all types of land.

Between local residents and tourists Farmers do not want tourists on their land; a new reservoir may flood farmland and people's homes; tourists want to use reservoirs for recreation and they want souvenir shops while residents need convenience shops; quarries provide work for locals but spoil the views for tourists; tourists want wider roads while residents want less traffic; there is not enough room for quarry traffic and coaches on narrow roads.

Between different groups of tourists Water skiers disturb people who want to fish, large groups of ramblers disturb bird-watchers, conservation groups conflict with visitors causing pollution and damage.

Should quarrying be allowed in National Parks?

Benefits Quarries provide an important source of employment and income. Better roads have to be built to accommodate large lorries. Local councils benefit from rates paid by the quarrying firms. Slate quarries provide roofing material, limestone quarries give lime for fertiliser and cement (photo **C**) – both create wealth for the local community and the nation.

Problems Quarries cause considerable pollution and damage the environment. Dust is created during blasting operations. Noise is caused by both blasting and heavy lorries. Visual pollution results from ugly buildings, spoil heaps and scarred hillsides (photo **C**). Traffic congestion can be caused by heavy lorries using roads that are too narrow.

National Park Authorities try to ensure that working quarries are landscaped and screened, while old quarries are restored, whenever possible, to their pre-quarry appearance after the mineral has been extracted.

C Visual pollution caused by quarrying in the Yorkshire Dales

Activities

1 a) Why were National Parks set up?
   b) What are the main tasks of the National Park Authorities?
   c) How can conflicts occur in National Parks between:
      i) different land users
      ii) residents and tourists
      iii) different groups of tourists?

2 For any one economic activity found in a National Park:
   a) describe how it benefits the local community
   b) describe how it can harm the environment.

3 Copy and complete diagram **D** by adding labels to show how quarries can reduce damage to the environment:
   a) when they are working
   b) after quarrying has finished.

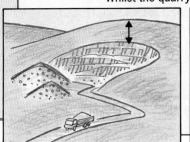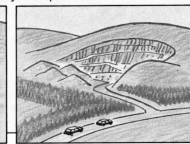
D Whilst the quarry is in operation | After quarrying has finished

Summary

Conflicting demands can occur in National Parks and other areas of considerable scenic attraction.

How can tourists spoil the environment?

A Bowness, 1832

B

- Improved access by M6 and local road improvements
- More leisure time due to shorter working weeks, part-time jobs and earlier retirement
- Advertising on TV and in magazines. Emphasis on need to relax, health and exercise
- More people have longer and paid holidays
- Greater mobility, more people own cars. 23 million people live within 3 hours' drive of Bowness
- Self-catering holidays, camping and caravanning

Bowness – a Lake District honeypot

C Lake Windermere

By providing leisure amenities for tourists visiting areas of outstanding scenic attraction, it is possible to damage the environment which first attracted people to it. For example:

- the building of tall hotel blocks in Mediterranean coastal areas has hidden the spectacular views of mountains which rise behind many of the resorts
- the construction of ski lifts has damaged mountainous areas
- the addition of tourist facilities and leisure amenities has affected the English Lake District.

Bowness is located on Lake Windermere. Its scenic environment has attracted visitors for many generations (picture **A**). The first tourists enjoyed mainly **passive activities** such as relaxing and admiring the views of the lake and the mountains. There was plenty of opportunity to wander through unspoilt woodland and to observe local wildlife. As time progressed visitors turned increasingly to more **active pursuits** such as water sports, fell walking and rock climbing. Even though more amenities were added for the comfort and enjoyment of the tourist, Bowness continued to maintain its attractive environment. Consequently it became an increasingly popular place to visit. Some of the reasons for this increased popularity are given in diagram **B**. Today, especially at weekends in summer, Bowness has become a 'honeypot' (photos **C** and **D**). A honeypot is a place of attractive scenery, or of historic interest, to which tourists swarm in large numbers. The problem is, 'How can the honeypot's natural beauty, the reason for it attracting so many people, be preserved while providing facilities for the numerous peak-time visitors?' If the environment becomes too overcrowded or damaged, people will turn away and visit other places.

D Bowness, 1993

Threats to the environment – especially at certain times of the week and year

- Any large increase in the number of tourists will reduce the peacefulness of the area, and is likely to increase the problems of litter and vandalism.
- An increase in cars and tourist coaches means congestion on narrow roads leading into Bowness, congestion where several roads meet in the centre of Bowness, a bottleneck at the ferry, problems of car parking, and an increase in noise and fumes from traffic.
- Lake Windermere is becoming overused. As there is freedom of navigation on the lake, some 1500 vessels may use it on a summer Bank Holiday weekend. There is competition between people wanting to use canoes, yachts, speedboats and lake steamers, and those wanting to windsurf, water-ski, fish or just enjoy the wildlife.
- Bowness itself becomes overcrowded. Cafés and car parks fill up, and local shops either have to put up prices or become souvenir shops.
- Views of the lake and mountains are spoilt by increased house building and enlarged caravan parks and camp sites.
- In winter, hotels, cafés and souvenir shops may have to close and second homes are left unoccupied.

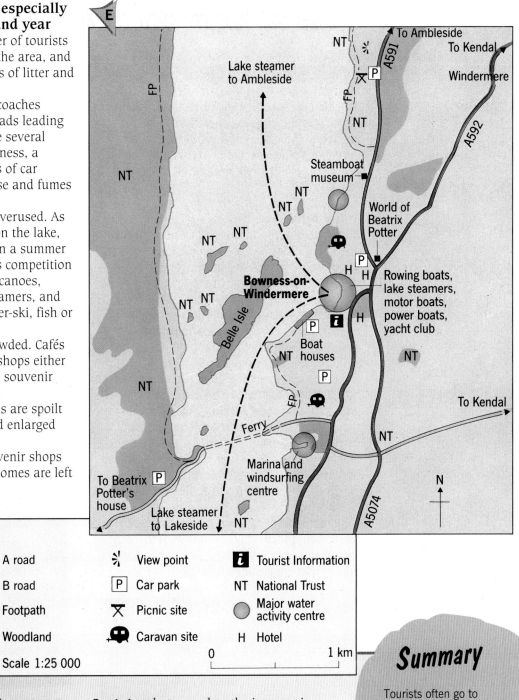

Key

————	A road	⚡	View point	ℹ️	Tourist Information
═══════	B road	P	Car park	NT	National Trust
– – FP – –	Footpath	✕	Picnic site	🔵	Major water activity centre
🪨	Woodland	🚐	Caravan site	H	Hotel
	Scale 1:25 000	0		1 km	

Activities

1 a) Why is the Lake District environment a source of attraction?
   b) Why are visitors to Bowness, on Lake Windermere, increasing in number?
   c) Refer to map **E**. What leisure amenities have been added to help visitors enjoy:
      i)   the lake
      ii) the lakeside
      iii) the views
      iv) a wet day?

2 a) In what ways has the increase in leisure activities harmed the very environment which was the source of their attraction?
   b) Table **F** is the result of a survey of tourists who were making a return visit to Bowness. Do you think Bowness has been completely spoilt or not? Give reasons for your opinion.

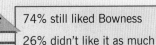

74% still liked Bowness	10.2% thought it had become too commercialised
26% didn't like it as much	15.3% thought it had become too crowded

Summary

Tourists often go to places of great scenic beauty, such as snow-covered mountains, sandy beaches with warm seas, and lakes in mountainous areas, to join in leisure activities. Without care and planning, these leisure activities can damage the environment that was the original source of their attraction.

▷ How can tourism increase soil erosion? ◁

Human activities can speed up the rate of several natural processes. In the case of tourism, this is most likely in areas of considerable scenic beauty and at honeypots. In both cases the large number of visitors can accelerate the rate of **soil erosion**. The most vulnerable places include mountains, where people can walk or ski, by lakes and along coastal cliffs.

Mountains

Footpaths Walking is the most popular active pastime in Britain. The most energetic walkers are those who climb mountains or use long-distance footpaths. Many of the most favoured walks are in fragile environments. Walkers on grassy paths, however careful they might be, trample and kill vegetation, and compress the underlying soil. When it rains the water cannot sink into the hardened ground. Where footpaths are on level ground, they will become boggy. Where they are on steeper slopes, water will drain into them forming small streams. As these small streams flow downhill they will carry soil with them. In both cases walkers will make detours to find drier ground. In doing so they will either create new routes or widen existing ones (photo **A**). In some parts of the North Yorkshire Moors, the peat has been compressed from two and a half metres to under half a metre. Parts of the Pennine Way long-distance footpath have been so badly eroded that suggestions have been made to pave parts of it, even if that would spoil its natural appearance.

Skiing There are now over 50 000 ski runs and 16 000 ski lifts in Europe. Tracts of forest have often been cleared to create new, longer and more challenging ski runs. These cleared paths form natural routes for avalanches and snow meltwater in spring, and for rainwater following storms in summer. Rocks and stones are carried downhill creating large gullies. Where skiing takes place on thin snow, the underlying vegetation dies, and there will be no roots to bind the soil together. As ski runs are on steep slopes, the downhill movement of material can be significant (photo **B**).

B Damage caused by ski runs

Lakesides

Less energetic walkers like to walk along the banks of lakes enjoying either the views or the wildlife. Here too grass becomes trampled and dies leaving the roots of trees and the soil exposed. Meanwhile, waves are created on the lake, especially where there are fast power boats or large pleasure boats. These waves travel towards the land, breaking as they reach the shore. The waves will erode and undercut the bank causing it to collapse and retreat (photo **C**).

A Footpath erosion on the Pennine Way

D Holbeck Hall Hotel, Scarborough

Coasts

The best views looking along the coast or out to sea are obtained from vantage points on the top of sea cliffs. Hotels have often been built on top of cliffs so that their owners can attract visitors by advertising 'a room with a sea view'. The weight of a hotel, however, adds pressure to a cliff, and some cliffs are not as stable as people sometimes imagine them to be. Following several dry summers, the early months of 1993 were very wet. As the top layer of part of a cliff at Scarborough became saturated it began to move, under gravity, downhill. One large hotel on the cliff top collapsed and also slid downhill (photo **D**).

Activities

1 How might tourists increase the rate of soil erosion in:
   a) mountainous parts of Britain in summer
   b) mountainous parts of Scotland in winter
   c) along the sides of lakes in the Lake District
   d) on coastal cliffs around Britain?

2 Choose phrases from the following list and place them in the appropriate boxes in flow diagram **E**.
   • *wear away grass* • *undercut banks*
   • *cause waves* • *walkers*

• *snow and rain channelled down paths* • *pleasure-boat operator*
• *rock and soil carried downhill* • *bank collapses* • *ski resort owner*
• *path cleared through trees* • *soil exposed* • *rain flows down footpaths*

3 a) Choose one of the four examples given in activity **1**. Describe carefully the methods you might use to try to reduce the damage and the rate of soil erosion caused by tourists visiting the area you have chosen.
   b) Give four other examples of how human activities may speed up natural processes.

E

[flow diagram] → **Increased soil erosion**

Summary

Leisure activities can harm the environment by significantly speeding up natural processes. One example is the increased rate of soil erosion caused by tourists visiting areas of considerable scenic attraction.

How do growing populations put pressure on natural resources?

Each environment is considered to have a saturation point where the total population equals its **carrying capacity**. The carrying capacity is the total population, which can be wildlife as well as people, that can be supported by the natural resources of that environment. As populations increase, extra pressure is put upon the existing resources.

Kenya has one of the highest birth rates in the world. As its population increases so too does the need to produce more food. Two of Kenya's most valuable resources are its varied, attractive landscapes and its wildlife. Both resources attract tourists from overseas, and tourists spend money. But there is a conflict of interest. As Kenya tries to increase the amount of land under crops, farming encroaches upon the landscape and wildlife habitats. Caught up in this conflict is the elephant. The elephant is considered to be essential for the tourist industry (a natural resource) but its existence and the recent increase in numbers (population) threaten Kenya's farmers.

A Elephants at Tsavo National Park

B Elephants creating a waterhole

The elephant as an important natural resource

Tourism is Kenya's main source of overseas income. Over 50 per cent of tourists spend their whole holiday in beach resorts. The remainder travel inland, usually on safaris, hoping to see as much wildlife as possible. The greatest expectation on a safari is to see elephants. The most popular National Parks and Game Reserves are those where sightings of elephants can be guaranteed (photo **A**). But elephants are also essential to the ecosystem. They can 'smell' underground water during dry seasons and in times of drought. By digging with their feet and trunks (photo **B**) they create water holes which attract, and keep alive, many other types of wildlife.

The elephant as a threat

To many African farmers, elephants are animals to be feared – partly because they do occasionally kill people, but mainly because of the damage they do to crops. Much of southern Kenya is intensively cultivated with individual shambas (farms) often only one or two hectares in size (photo **D**). The shambas may be surrounded by small thicket fences, but these are no protection against a herd of elephants – and a herd trampling across a shamba will flatten and ruin any crop. Farmers also need water for their own needs and their cattle. One large bull elephant can drink 100 litres in one bout and 200 litres in a day – another source of conflict between farmer and animal. Elephants also eat for 19 hours a day. In the rainy season they eat leaves. As it gets increasingly drier and there are fewer leaves, they first eat the stems and finally the roots of plants. To obtain roots elephants have to uproot whole trees. The result is a short-term destruction of the environment.

The elephant under threat

During the early 1970s relatively large numbers of elephants died due to a severe drought. During the 1980s eight out of every ten elephants in Kenya were killed by poachers wanting ivory. In October 1989 CITES (the Convention on International Trade in Endangered Species) managed to get a global agreement which outlawed the trafficking of ivory. The elephant population is slowly beginning to rise again – although it still remains well below its carrying capacity. The same cannot be said for Kenya's human population. Kenya has one of the highest birth rates in the world, and its population is increasing rapidly. More people means more crops, and more crops means less land for elephants and other wildlife. Slowly the natural habitats for wildlife are being destroyed.

Elephants under control

Attempts are being made to erect electric fences around farming areas to try to segregate elephants from farmland. Corridors are left through farming areas to allow elephants to migrate. Farmers are being encouraged to view elephants as an important resource. In return they are now beginning to receive some of the income obtained through tourism (previously local people did not benefit financially from tourists). Now that poaching seems defeated, elephants are being encouraged to spread out. This is widening the viewing areas for tourists and is enabling more local communities to benefit. Elephant numbers are now growing sufficiently rapidly for wildlife workers to be investigating methods of contraception among females in the herd. Such a policy is preferential to the alternative of possible future cullings as a means of controlling numbers.

C
Burning confiscated ivory, Kenya

D Shambas in southern Kenya

Activities

E

1 Look at graph **E**.
   a) Why did the elephant population decrease in the:
      i) early 1970s
      ii) 1980s?
   b) Why did the elephant population begin to increase after October 1989?

2 Why are elephants important to Kenya's:
   a) economy
   b) natural environment?

3 **a)** Why is there conflict between farmers and elephants?
   b) How is this conflict being resolved?

Number of elephants in Kenya (thousands)

130
125
100
75 — 65
50
25 — 16 — 26 — 34
0
1973   1978   1983   1988   1993   96

Summary In those parts of the world where there is a rapid growth in population, there is usually an equally rapid increase in pressure on natural resources.

159

Case Study A

Coastal management – part of the Wessex coast

What are the problems facing this stretch of coastline?

The coastline between the towering cliffs at Durlston Head (Dorset) and the low-lying spit at Hurst Castle (Hampshire) is shown on map **A**. Like most other coastlines in Britain it is dynamic and always changing. These changes are caused by:

◆ natural (physical) processes of weather, waves and tides
◆ human intervention and activity.

The problems created by these changes vary from one part of the coastline to another (places A to F on map **A**).

A Swanage Bay

This stretch of coastline is relatively stable apart from some erosion of the softer clay cliffs south of Ballard Point (diagram **B** page 48). The adjacent limestone and chalk cliffs form a habitat for birds and lime-loving plants (photo **E** page 23). Most of the problems in this area result from the settlement at Swanage and the influx of tourists in summer. Coastal footpaths become eroded, litter is left, and there is some sewage outflow into the sea.

B South Haven peninsula and Poole Harbour

The peninsula is a major sand dune ecosystem (habitat) which is slowly growing seawards (photo **B**). Behind it are salt and freshwater marsh (wetlands), and heath and woodland ecosystems noted for their seabirds, wildfowl, lizards and butterflies. The main problem is tourists, with over one million people a year trampling over the fragile South Haven dunes. Poole Harbour is also threatened by pollution from a freight and cross-Channel terminal as well as from several marinas.

C Bournemouth

Bournemouth is a major tourist resort built on top of cliffs. There is little natural coastline left and wildlife habitats are limited. The sea is affected by some sewage outflow, the hotels add pressure to the cliffs, and tourists and residents create noise and litter.

D Hengistbury Head and Christchurch Harbour

The headland and harbour consist of several wildlife habitats – salt marsh, freshwater marsh, heath, sand dunes and rocky foreshore – all with an abundance of wildlife (photo **C**). The harbour suffers from silting and water sports.

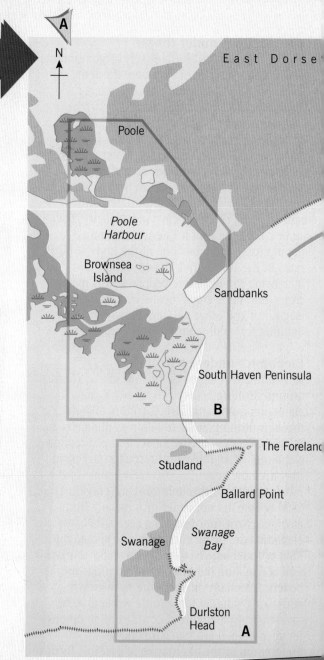

Sand dunes at South Haven

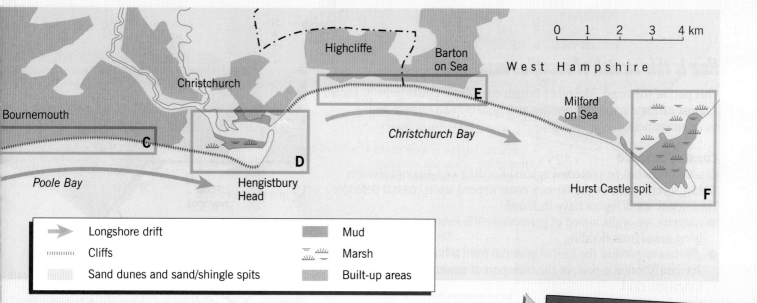

Legend:
- → Longshore drift
- ···· Cliffs
- Sand dunes and sand/shingle spits
- Mud
- Marsh
- Built-up areas

Map labels: Bournemouth, Christchurch, Highcliffe, Barton on Sea, West Hampshire, Milford on Sea, Poole Bay, Christchurch Bay, Hengistbury Head, Hurst Castle spit

Scale: 0 1 2 3 4 km

Markers: C, D, E, F

E Christchurch Bay

The 30 metre high cliffs between Highcliffe and Barton on Sea have retreated by over 60 metres since 1971. The sand and clay cliffs readily become waterlogged after heavy rain, causing mudflows and landslips (photo **D**). This material is then removed by waves, especially during storms and at high tide.

F Hurst Castle spit

The shingle spit was formed by eroded cliff material from Christchurch Bay being carried eastwards by longshore drift (diagram **A** page 24 and pages 26–27). Before 1954 the spit was never breached by the sea. Since then, however, the supply of material has been reduced by the introduction of groynes to the west (photo **B** page 24). This, together with the increased frequency and intensity of storms and higher tides (attributed to global warming), has meant that the spit is now breached by the sea several times a year. The spit, with its sand dunes and salt marsh behind, is an important wildlife habitat – but a habitat with a threatened existence.

D Landslip near Barton on Sea

C Hengistbury Head and coast protection

Activities

1 Using pages 22–23, 26–27, 48 and 160–161, describe how the coastal landforms in Swanage Bay (A on map **A**) differ from those at Hurst Castle (F on map **A**).

2 a) Which parts of the coast shown on map **A** experience the greatest:
   i) natural (physical) problems
   ii) human problems?
   b) Give a brief description of these problems.

Summary
Coastlines are dynamic and constantly changing. These changes, which may be due to natural processes or to human activity, can create problems.

A volcanic eruption — Ruapehu, New Zealand

New Zealand's volcanoes are part of the **'ring of fire'**, a chain of mountains that fringes the Pacific Ocean (map **B** page 52). These mountains coincide with the boundary of the Pacific Plate and several neighbouring plates (map **A** page 54). Approximately three-quarters of the Earth's active volcanoes occur along the various Pacific Plate boundaries.

New Zealand lies on a destructive plate boundary (page 54). Here heavier oceanic crust of the Pacific Plate is forced downwards on contact with the lighter continental crust of the Indo-Australian Plate (map **A**). As the Pacific Plate descends into the mantle, a process known as **subduction**, it enters an area of intense heat and enormous pressure (diagram **B**). Friction between the two plates causes the oceanic crust to melt and to be destroyed.

This results in, at a depth of 75 to 150 km, the formation of mixture of molten rock and gases known as **magma**. As magma is less dense than the surrounding material, it rises. Where there are weaknesses in the crust, magma is able to force its way onto the Earth's surface where it can form volcanoes.

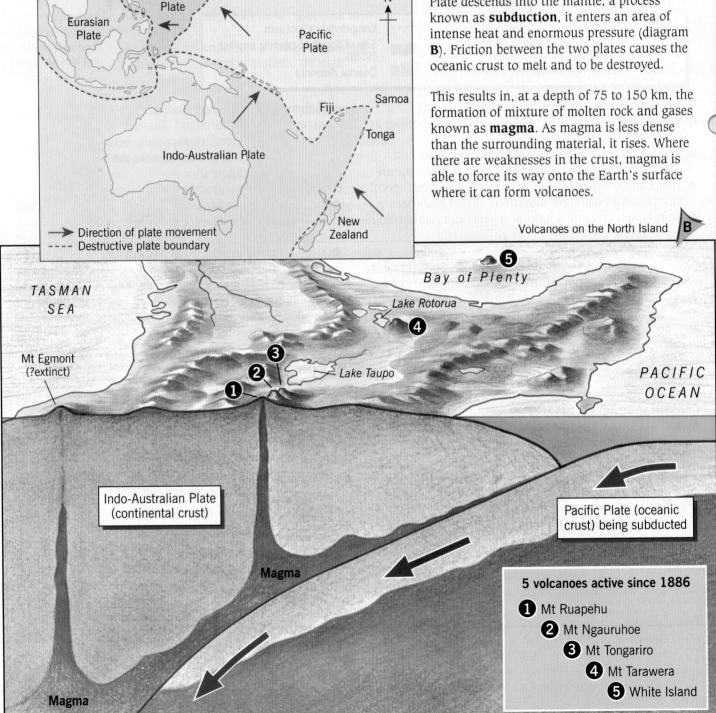

A Plates in the south-west Pacific

Eurasian Plate

Philippines Plate

Pacific Plate

N

Fiji

Samoa

Tonga

Indo-Australian Plate

New Zealand

→ Direction of plate movement

- - - Destructive plate boundary

B Volcanoes on the North Island

TASMAN SEA

Bay of Plenty

Lake Rotorua

❹

Mt Egmont (?extinct)

❸

❷

❶

Lake Taupo

PACIFIC OCEAN

Indo-Australian Plate (continental crust)

Magma

Pacific Plate (oceanic crust) being subducted

Magma

5 volcanoes active since 1886

❶ Mt Ruapehu

❷ Mt Ngauruhoe

❸ Mt Tongariro

❹ Mt Tarawera

❺ White Island

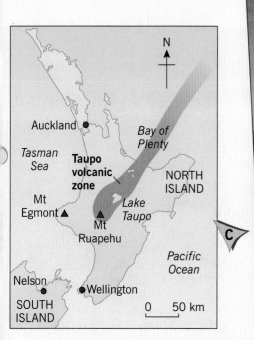

D The summit of Ruapehu

There are several geothermal areas within the 240 km long Taupo Volcanic Zone of New Zealand's North Island (map **C**). Also located within this narrow zone are five volcanoes which have erupted since 1886. Of these Ruapehu, in the Tongariro National Park, is the largest (photo **D**). Over the last million years Ruapehu and its neighbours have been built up from successive eruptions. Some of these eruptions have been explosive, sending ash and rock into the sky. Others have been quieter, allowing lava to flow more gently from the crater. Ruapehu's summit (2797 m) is high enough to be permanently snow-covered, and for its upper slopes to include seven small glaciers (the longest is 1.8 km).

Within Ruapehu's crater is a lake 500 m wide. This lake is a major cause of **lahars**. *Lahar* is an Indonesian word describing mudflows on volcanoes. They are caused by water-saturated volcanic debris moving downslope at speeds of up to 80 km per hour under the influence of gravity. They occur on Ruapehu when rising magma heats the water of the crater lake causing it to overflow. The heated water melts the surrounding snow and rushes downhill collecting ash and other debris deposited by earlier eruptions (photo **E**). In 1953, a lahar swept away a rail bridge over the Whangaehu

River at the foot of the mountain minutes before the arrival of the Auckland to Wellington express. The locomotive and six carriages plunged into the river killing 151 people.

E Active Ruapehu, September 1995

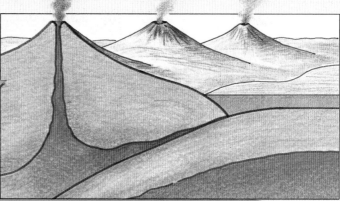

F

Activities

1 **a)** Explain why volcanoes occur on the North Island of New Zealand.
   b) Make a copy of diagram **F**. On it label:
   - *Pacific Plate* • *Indo-Australian Plate* • *oceanic crust*
   - *continental crust* • *Mt Ruapehu* • *Mt Ngauruhoe*
   - *Mt Tongariro*

2 **a)** What are lahars?
   b) Why can they be a hazard?

Summary

New Zealand lies on a destructive plate boundary. Ruapehu is the largest of five volcanoes which have erupted there since 1886.

A Eruption of Ruapehu, 1995

In 1995 and 1996 volcano lovers were treated to a touch of magic from a volcano lying at the heart of the central North Island of New Zealand. In September 1995 Ruapehu, 'the restless mountain', burst into life. The power of the ensuing eruptions captured world-wide attention as towering columns of ash and steam, torrential mudflows and incandescent lava bombs presented an ongoing spectacle (photo **A**).

However, while locally spectacular, on a global scale and in terms of Ruapehu's formative history, the latest eruptions were fairly insignificant – the eruption of Mount St Helens in the USA in 1980 was ten times bigger, and the climate-changing Philippine eruption of Mt Pinatubo in 1991 (page 56) was up to one hundred times larger. But, unlike St Helens or Pinatubo, Ruapehu, the highest mountain in the North Island (2979 m), is an extremely popular outdoor playground, attracting hundreds of thousands of skiers, climbers and sightseers each year (photo **B**).

The event

Late 1994	Hot gases from underlying magma rise through the rubble-filled vent towards the crater. Lake heats up.
1995	
Late June	Magma begins to rise up the vent.
29 June	Explosive eruptions progressively clear the vent.
23 September	Largest eruption finally clears the vent. Large rocks tossed up to a kilometre above the summit (photo **A**). Vertical ejection of ash and steam. The explosion, at the end of a busy ski day, is witnessed by thousands of people on the volcano (photo **B**). Further eruptions create lahars, one of which just misses the ski-lift (photo **C**).
25–30 September	Explosive activity virtually continuous. Larger eruptions almost empty the lake. Major lahars flow down the Whangaehu Valley. Sightseers watch from The Grand Chateau Hotel (photo **D**).
11 October	Main body of magma reaches surface. Molten lava and bombs ejected. Ash falls over central and eastern North Island.
Mid-October (to 1996)	Ash eruptions die down. Replaced by release of enormous amounts of steam. The gas causes a pale blue-brown haze (volcanic smog or **vog**). New lake begins to form in crater.
1996	
15–16 June	Intense volcanic tremors warn of more rising magma.
17 June	Major eruption produces huge ash clouds. The crater again empties of water. At night molten lava ejected as a fountain.
18 June and July	Moderate eruptions with some red hot rocks and much ash.
August and September	Occasional eruptions.
October	Gas and steam ejected intermittently as activity dies away.

B A ski lift on the slopes of Ruapehu

The effects

The western slopes of Ruapehu include a ski lodge, two ski-fields and Whakapapa village with its information centre and luxury hotel (photo **D**). Nearby are three small townships which have come to rely increasingly on skiing for their main source of income.

C Lahar flowing past a ski lift

◆ **Ash**
  • covered the ski-slopes (1995 and 1996) and lahars cut across ski-runs (1995) seriously disrupting two ski seasons
  • damaged turbines in a local hydro-electric power station
  • closed airports for several days in both years (ash can damage or stop aeroplane engines): domestic and international flights affected
  • in 1996 was so dense that is lowered temperatures by 5 to 10°C
  • caused some respiratory and eye problems
  • had to be washed off fruit trees
  • provided fresh phosphate (free), which should improve farming.
◆ **Mudflows** – choked several local rivers and killed fish.
◆ **Large boulders** (volcanic bombs) – damaged the Dome Shelter and caused minor snow avalanches on the upper slopes of Ruapehu.
◆ **Gases** – produced a pale blue-brown smog.
◆ **Eruption** – became a major tourist attraction.

D Eruption of Ruapehu behind The Grand Chateau Hotel, 17 June 1996

How can a future event be predicted?

◆ By studying pre-eruption activity to see if there are repeat patterns.
◆ By mapping ancient and recent lava and lahar flows to see if they follow specific routes.
◆ By using monitoring equipment to see if lake temperatures rise, pressure builds up, seismic activity (earth tremors) increase, the mountain's shape alters (as with Mount St Helens) or there are changes in the chemical composition of released gases and/or lake water.
◆ By setting up early warning systems, especially of lahars, and issuing warnings to skiers, walkers and visitors to the mountain.

Activities

1 a) Describe the main events of the 1995 and 1996 eruptions.
   b) How did these events affect:
       i) people's way of life, ii) the environment?

2 a) What can be done to predict future eruptions in the Ruapehu area?
   b) Why is it easier to predict eruptions in an economically more developed country like New Zealand than in an economically less developed country?

Summary

Volcanic eruptions can interrupt people's way of life and change their environment. Attempts are being made, with some success, to predict eruptions.

A transnational car company – Toyota

Transnational (multinational) corporations

Each transnational corporation has factories in several countries and operates regardless of national boundaries. Globally they employ millions of workers. The largest transnational corporations are usually oil companies such as Shell, Esso or Exxon, or car manufacturers such as General Motors, Ford and Toyota. General Motors is the largest transnational. Only about 20 countries in the world earn more money in a year than this single corporation does.

The car industry

Car firms were amongst the first to become transnationals. By taking advantage of making parts and manufacturing cars in several different countries (figure **A**), they became global organisations.

Any global location...

- Near to large centres of population (markets)
- Can afford to buy the best sites (land)
- Can afford to re-invest and to modernise
- Can afford to train and employ skilled labour

To get around local trade barriers

Encouraged by governments

An economically less developed country location...

- Uses the large amount of cheap labour
- Uses local raw materials – cheaper than transporting them to more developed countries
- Fewer trade union restrictions

A

The Japanese car industry in the UK

During the 1950s, the relatively small world car industry was mainly located in the USA and Britain (diagram **B**). In the late 1970s, however, Japanese cars began to flood the UK market as well as markets in the rest of Western Europe and in North America. This led to several governments, including those of Britain and the USA, making agreements with the Japanese. These agreements aimed at restricting the number of cars which could be imported. In the UK, for example, the Japanese were not allowed to sell more than 11 per cent of the UK's annual total car sales. Later, to try to overcome this barrier, three of the largest Japanese car manufacturers either:

- ◆ built their own car assembly plants in the UK, e.g. Nissan at Washington and Toyota at Burnaston, or
- ◆ amalgamated with existing British car manufacturers, e.g. Honda with Rover at Swindon.

B

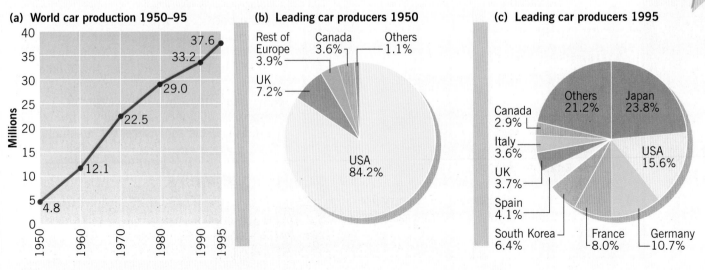

(a) World car production 1950–95

(Millions)
- 1950: 4.8
- 1960: 12.1
- 1970: 22.5
- 1980: 29.0
- 1990: 33.2
- 1995: 37.6

(b) Leading car producers 1950

- Rest of Europe 3.9%
- Canada 3.6%
- Others 1.1%
- UK 7.2%
- USA 84.2%

(c) Leading car producers 1995

- Others 21.2%
- Japan 23.8%
- Canada 2.9%
- Italy 3.6%
- UK 3.7%
- Spain 4.1%
- South Korea 6.4%
- France 8.0%
- Germany 10.7%
- USA 15.6%

Toyota in the UK

Toyota is the world's third largest manufacturer of cars. It is by far the largest manufacturer whose parent company has its head office in Japan. It manufactures 4.6 million cars world-wide. This is the equivalent of one car produced every six seconds, and one car in every eight produced (diagram **Ba**).

Europe is the world's largest market for cars. Toyota decided, therefore, that it was essential to locate a vehicle manufacturing plant within that market. In December 1989 the company announced that the plant would be located at Burnaston in the UK. The UK was chosen, according to Toyota, because it had:
◆ a large domestic market of its own
◆ a long tradition in vehicle manufacture (diagram **Bb**)

◆ a skilled and flexible work force
◆ many firms already making car components
◆ good communications with the rest of Europe
◆ an encouraging government both at local and national levels.

Burnaston, in Derbyshire (map **C**), was selected because:
◆ it was on flat land of a former airfield and farms
◆ the land was relatively cheap to buy
◆ it had a greenfield location with room for future expansion (photo **D**)
◆ it was central to the UK domestic market
◆ it was close to the West Midlands and therefore close to many parts suppliers.

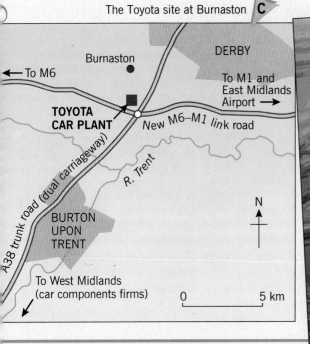

The Toyota site at Burnaston **C**

D Burnaston, Derbyshire

Activities

1 **a)** What is a transnational company?
   b) Why did car manufacturers become transnationals?

2 **a)** Make a sketch of photo **D**. On it label its advantages for the location of a car plant.
   b) Using the headings in diagram **E**, explain why Toyota chose:
   i) the UK ii) Burnaston
   as the location for its European car assembly plant.

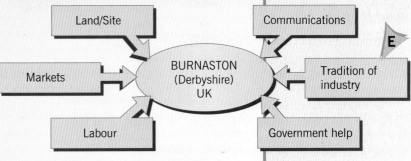

E

Land/Site → BURNASTON (Derbyshire) UK ← Communications
Markets → BURNASTON (Derbyshire) UK ← Tradition of industry
Labour → BURNASTON (Derbyshire) UK ← Government help

Summary Toyota is an example of a transnational (global) company with factories in several countries. Burnaston (Derbyshire) was chosen as the location for the company's first European car plant.

Toyota today

Toyota Motor Manufacturing (UK) Ltd has two factories – its engine plant in Deeside in North Wales and the vehicle manufacturing plant at Burnaston, Derbyshire (table **A**). Approximately 70 per cent of production goes to Europe and 10 per cent to 70 countries world-wide. The remaining 20 per cent stays in the UK.

Part of the agreement to allow Toyota to locate in the UK was that 80 per cent of the car must be local content. To meet this target, Toyota must buy parts from European suppliers. By 1996 Toyota was using over 200 suppliers from 11 European countries, of which over half were UK-based (map **B**). Local suppliers support Toyota's 'just-in-time' (JIT) policy, which is now used by many other firms. JIT means using the minimum amount of resources in the most efficient way, e.g. component parts are delivered as they are needed as this avoids expensive storage and supports good quality.

Toyota is a fully integrated operation. It includes technical training, the manufacturing of component parts, the assembly of those parts on a production line (figure **C**), and finally the marketing, sales, distribution and post-sales service.

A Toyota Motor Manufacturing (UK) Ltd

	Employees		Car production
Location	Engine plant, Deeside	Assembly plant, Burnaston	–
1996	172	2050	110 000 (one assembly plant)
1998	200	3000	200 000 (two assembly plants)

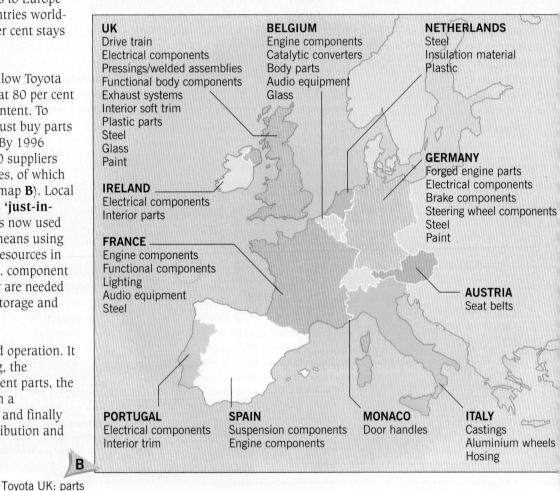

UK
Drive train
Electrical components
Pressings/welded assemblies
Functional body components
Exhaust systems
Interior soft trim
Plastic parts
Steel
Glass
Paint

IRELAND
Electrical components
Interior parts

FRANCE
Engine components
Functional components
Lighting
Audio equipment
Steel

BELGIUM
Engine components
Catalytic converters
Body parts
Audio equipment
Glass

NETHERLANDS
Steel
Insulation material
Plastic

GERMANY
Forged engine parts
Electrical components
Brake components
Steering wheel components
Steel
Paint

AUSTRIA
Seat belts

PORTUGAL
Electrical components
Interior trim

SPAIN
Suspension components
Engine components

MONACO
Door handles

ITALY
Castings
Aluminium wheels
Hosing

B Toyota UK: parts and raw materials

What is TPS?

The **Toyota Production System (TPS)** forms the basis of the corporation's success. Its three main aims are:
1 *For the customer* – the highest-quality product, at the lowest possible cost and greatest value for money, and in the shortest possible lead-time.
2 *For the workforce* – work satisfaction, job security and fair treatment.
3 *For the company* – the smoothest possible works operation, with least waste and error, with market flexibility and maximum profit.
These aims are achieved through *jidoka*, just-in-time and *kaizen*.

Jidoka prevents mistakes from happening, stops production automatically should a problem develop, and enables immediate solutions to be put into effect.

Just-in-time provides each process in the car assembly sequence with only the types and quantities of components required and at exactly the time when they are needed. This approach prevents the accumulation of parts and the excessive production of any item.

Kaizen is the continuing improvements that work teams and their leaders make in trying to streamline the flow of work, enhance quality and improve working conditions. It is a dynamic process aimed at making the assembly line more efficient and enjoyable.

1 Raw steel is checked for quality, presses shape the body panels, panels are transferred to the weld shop.

2 Robots then weld the body shell together. The shell is thoroughly cleaned.

3 Paint is cured in ovens. Bumpers and fascias are moulded in plastic. Every engine is hot-tested.

4 In assembly, 2500 parts are fitted.

Activities

1 **a)** Why are 80 per cent of the parts for the Toyota factory at Burnaston made within the EU?

   b) Why do over half of these parts come from within the UK?

2 **a)** How does the Toyota Production System aim to help
   i) customers ii) the workforce
   iii) the company?

   b) How do the headlines in diagram **D** help fulfil these aims?

3 **a)** What is an assembly line?

   b) Describe the main stages in the Toyota assembly line.

JIDOKA

KAIZEN

D

JUST-IN-TIME

Summary

Toyota aims to provide the highest-quality product at the lowest possible cost and in the shortest time.

Case Study D

The cycle of industrial change — Teesside

The growth of industry (1850–1980)

Teesside's industrial development began in the 1850s immediately after the discovery of ironstone at Easton in the nearby Cleveland Hills (map **A**). Within three years there were 35 blast furnaces in the area. Teesside had several advantages for the location of industry.

◆ Near to the basic raw materials:

- For early iron production and later, after 1876, steel-making (coal from Durham, iron ore from the Cleveland Hills and limestone from the Pennines). By 1950, 30 per cent of pig iron produced in the UK came from Teesside.
- For chemical industry (rock salt from the Tees estuary).

◆ A tidewater site for importing raw materials (e.g. iron ore when local ores became exhausted, oil for the chemical industry) and the export of finished goods (e.g. ships, bridges, locomotives and machinery).

◆ Large areas of flat, marshy land which was cheap to buy and easy to reclaim either for docks or as sites for large factories (map **A**).

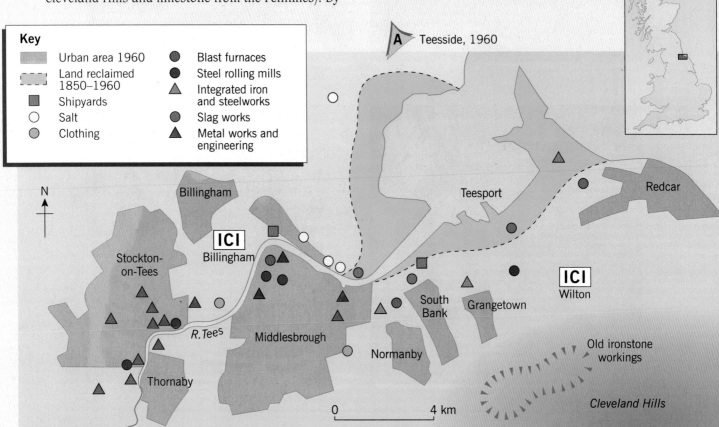

A Teesside, 1960

Key

- Urban area 1960
- Land reclaimed 1850–1960
- Shipyards
- Salt
- Clothing
- Blast furnaces
- Steel rolling mills
- Integrated iron and steelworks
- Slag works
- Metal works and engineering

Billingham · ICI · Billingham · Stockton-on-Tees · R. Tees · Middlesbrough · Thornaby · Normanby · South Bank · Grangetown · Teesport · Redcar · ICI Wilton · Old ironstone workings · Cleveland Hills

0 — 4 km

B ICI Wilton Works

During the 1960s, Teesside was regarded as 'the industrial centre of the future'. Successive governments helped modernise both the steel industry (nationalised in 1967) and the chemical industry (diagram **E**). A large, modern, integrated iron and steel works was opened at Redcar (map **C** page 141), and the Shell oil refinery at Teesport. At the same time, the expansion of ICI (Imperial Chemical Industries) continued (photo **B**). Indeed a major reason for creating Kielder Reservoir was the expected demand for water by Teesside. Unemployment fell to 2 per cent and 'full employment' seemed to be guaranteed.

The decline of industry (1980s)

The post-1974 oil price rises led to a world economic recession by the early 1980s. This recession had a major impact upon Teesside's main industries.

◆ The chemical industry, heavily dependent upon oil, saw job losses and the closure of the Teesport refinery (1984).

◆ A global fall in the demand for steel and improvements in technology caused British Steel to reduce its workforce from 30 000 in the early 1970s to under 5000 by 1990. Only the large Redcar works remained open.

◆ Shipbuilding was affected by the fall in steel production, the decline in world trade and competition from shipyards in Asia. Locomotive production ceased as road transport increasingly took over from rail.

◆ Employment in metal-using industries and in engineering also declined.

By 1987, 25 per cent of the Teesside workforce was unemployed. The traditional manufacturing industries had declined rapidly and the promised growth in service industries had not occurred (diagram **E**). The area was suffering from high unemployment (much of it long-term), dereliction of land and buildings caused by industrial decline, and from environmental pollution (photo **C**).

The British government and the European Regional Development Fund did provide some financial aid. However, new industries that were needed to replace the thousands of jobs lost, the retraining of people for those new types of job, and the conversion of land for the new industries, could not be achieved overnight. The problem was highlighted when newspapers showed a photograph of the then Prime Minister, Margaret Thatcher, walking across a wasteland site on Teesside (photo **D**).

C Teesside in the late 1980s

D Prime Minister Margaret Thatcher walks across a wasteland site on Teesside that is to be transformed by a TDC regeneration scheme (1987)

Activities

1 a) Give six reasons why Teesside became important for the production of iron and steel.
   b) What other industries were attracted to Teesside?

2 a) How are the two graphs in **E** different?
   b) What are the main differences between photo **B** and photos **C** and **D**?
   c) Give reasons for your answers to a) and b).

E

1966
- Primary 1.8%
- Chemicals 19.4%
- Services 40.5%
- Secondary 57.7%
- Metal manufacturing 19.0%
- Other manufacturing 9.8%
- Mechanical engineering and shipbuilding 9.5%

Unemployment 2%

1987
- Primary 2.4%
- Services 46.8%
- Secondary (industry) 50.8%

Unemployment 25%

Summary After a century of industrial growth, Teesside in the 1960s was seen as a major European centre of the future. By the late 1980s it had become an unemployment black spot.

173

Teesside in the 1990s

The Teesside Development Corporation (TDC) was set up in early 1987. It was given a high profile by Margaret Thatcher's much-publicised walk (photo **D** page 173). The TDC covered 4500 hectares of land along the banks of the Rives Tees and at Hartlepool. Of this land, almost one-quarter was either derelict or underused. The new emphasis was on two types of development:

1 • private-sector property development
  • public-financed redevelopment of former industrial sites by the TDC
2 projects aimed more towards the leisure and service sector rather than at the traditional work and manufacturing sector.

Fact file **A** lists the achievements of the TDC by 1996. Major projects completed by the TDC by that date included:

◆ Teesdale – a £500 million development with a mix of offices, housing, shops and leisure facilities (photo **B**). It is built around a series of canals.
◆ Teesside Park – a major retail and leisure complex now in its second phase of development.
◆ Tees Offshore Base – the first three phases of development have transformed a derelict shipyard into a centre of excellence in offshore technology with the creation of nearly 1400 jobs (photo **C**).
◆ Riverside Park – the new home of Middlesbrough Football Club.
◆ Hartlepool Marina – 80 ha of Hartlepool's South Dock have been converted into a leisure, retail and commercial area.
◆ A barrage across the River Tees will prevent flooding and improve water quality and water activities (maps **D**).

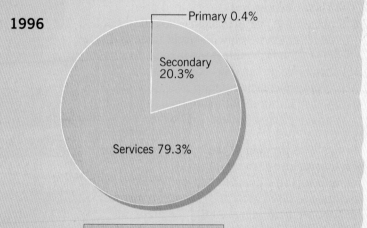

A

Fact file – TDC 1987–96

◆ Land reclaimed 386 hectares
◆ Housing units completed 1210
◆ Roads, built or improved 25 km
◆ Gross gain in permanent jobs 22 112
◆ Private-sector investment £1.2 billion
◆ Drop in unemployment 7%

1996

Primary 0.4%
Secondary 20.3%
Services 79.3%

Unemployment 18%

B Teesdale

C Tees Offshore Base

A cleaner Tees

A major clean-up of the River Tees and a boost to industrial development on Teesside will result from the Tees Estuary Environmental Scheme (TEES). TEES is a response by Northumbria Water, ICI and the industries of Wilton and Seal Sands, to the increasingly high EU environmental standards (maps **D**). Under the European Urban Waste Water Treatment Directive:

◆ Northumbria Water must provide further treatment for wastewater at present being discharged from its three sewage treatment works on Teesside

◆ major industries on Teesside must reduce their effluent flowing into the Tees.

New pipelines will be laid on both the north and the south sides of the river. These will take sewage and industrial effluent to a combined new treatment works on land provided by ICI. The scheme, which should be completed by 2002, will build upon improvements in water quality of the Tees already made in the last 25 years (maps **D**).

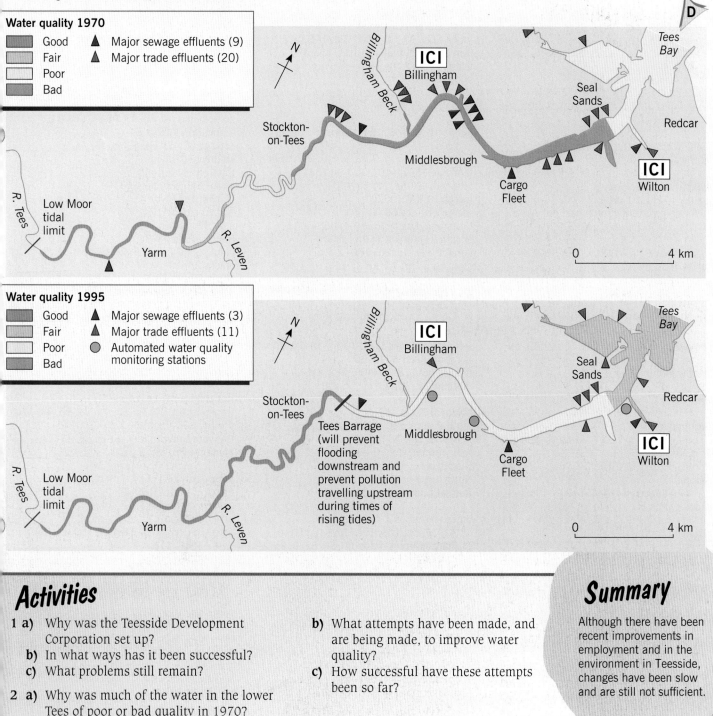

D

Water quality 1970
- Good
- Fair
- Poor
- Bad
- ▲ Major sewage effluents (9)
- ▲ Major trade effluents (20)

Water quality 1995
- Good
- Fair
- Poor
- Bad
- ▲ Major sewage effluents (3)
- ▲ Major trade effluents (11)
- ● Automated water quality monitoring stations

Tees Barrage (will prevent flooding downstream and prevent pollution travelling upstream during times of rising tides)

Activities

1 a) Why was the Teesside Development Corporation set up?

b) In what ways has it been successful?

c) What problems still remain?

2 a) Why was much of the water in the lower Tees of poor or bad quality in 1970?

b) What attempts have been made, and are being made, to improve water quality?

c) How successful have these attempts been so far?

Summary

Although there have been recent improvements in employment and in the environment in Teesside, changes have been slow and are still not sufficient.

Index

accessibility 96, 104, 123
Amazon, River 5, 8
arêtes 40, 41

Bangladesh 11, 16, 29, 64
bars 27
bays 22, 48
beaches 24–5, 26, 27, 150
birth rates 66–9, 70, 74, 134, 158, 159
Bowness, Lake District 154–5
Brazil 4, 63, 68, 71, 118–19, 129
business paks 95, 138, 139

Calcutta 74, 92–3
car industry 168–71
caves 23, 45, 48
CBD (central business district) 94–5, 138, 144–6
chemical weathering 44
cliffs 22, 24, 25, 48, 157
coal and coalfields 108, 116, 128, 132, 136–7, 141
coasts 22–31, 157, 160–3
Common Agricultural Policy (CAP) 124, 125
corries 38–9, 40, 41

death rates 66–7, 68–9, 70
deltas 10, 11, 31, 61
demographic transition model 66, 70
deposition 9–11, 26–7, 42–3

earthquakes 50, 51, 52–5, 56, 58–9, 60–1, 64
economic development 108–9, 117, 118, 132, 134–5, 142–3
electricity 132–3, 137, 140
employment structures 93, 116–19
energy sources 128–35
erosion 6–8, 22–3, 26, 31, 38–41, 43, 48
erratics 42
ethnic groups 78–9, 90, 91
EU 36, 122, 124–5
evapotranspiration 14

farm pollution 32, 34–5, 127
farming 11, 116, 120–7; farming systems 120–1
fertiliser 32, 126, 127, 153
fjords 30
flood hydrographs 14–15, 17
flood plains 10, 11, 18, 19
floods 8, 10–11, 12, 15, 16–21, 28–9, 114
France 63, 68, 71, 107
freeze–thaw 38
functional zones 94–5

Ganges, River 33
Germany 68, 107
glacial troughs 30, 40, 41, 42
glaciation 30, 38–43
global warming 31, 57, 132, 133, 134
government policies 100–1, 122–3

hanging valleys 41
headlands 22, 48

hedgerows 126
hierarchies 88–9, 144
honeypots 46, 154
housing 86, 90, 92, 94–5, 97, 98, 99, 100, 101, 138
hydro-electricity 20, 21, 128, 129, 132, 133
hydrological (water) cycle 12–13, 38

India 29, 63, 68, 69, 70–1, 118–19, 134
industrial pollution 32, 33, 34–5, 36, 37
industry 64, 65, 73, 96, 100, 101, 108, 116, 136–41, 168–75; see also employment structures
infant mortality 68
information technology (IT) 108
inner cities 95, 98–101, 138, 145, 147
iron and steel industry 108, 136, 141
Isle of Purbeck 48, 49
Israel 76–7

Japan 50, 63, 68, 74, 75

Kenya 10, 63, 68, 109, 129, 135, 142–3, 150–1, 158–9

land use 16, 94–101, 124–5, 138
land values 96, 138, 147
levées 10, 18, 19, 20
life expectancy 68
limestone (karst) 16, 44–7, 48, 49, 153
Location Quotient 119
London's Docklands 100–1
longshore drift 24, 26

map skills 80–3
meanders 8–9, 20
migration 70, 76–7, 78
mining 116, 132
Mississippi River 5, 8, 10, 11, 18–19, 20
Missouri River 5, 18, 20
models 66–7, 86, 94–5, 138
moraine 38, 39, 42

National Parks 152–3
natural resources 128–9, 142–3, 150, 158
networks 104–5
New York 90–1
Nile, River 5, 10, 11
North Sea 34, 35, 36–7, 130
nuclear power 128, 132, 133

offices 95, 96, 97, 108, 138
oil 34, 35, 36, 108, 128, 130–1, 137
Ordnance Survey maps 11, 80, 82–3, 85, 87, 104, 114–15
overpopulation 74–5, 134
oxbow lakes 8–9

planning 100–3, 111, 150–2, 159
plates and plate boundaries 53, 54–5, 56, 58, 61
pollution 32–7, 91, 98, 99, 106, 110–11, 127, 128, 130–1, 134, 150, 153
population 62–79, 129, 134–5, 158–9
population pyramids 70–1, 73

ports 108, 137
power stations 32, 132, 134, 140
precipitation 12, 13, 14–15, 16, 38
pyramidal peak 40, 41

quarrying 153

reservoirs 13, 18, 20, 21, 133
Rhine, River 33, 34, 36
rias 30
ribbon lakes 42, 43
ridge and vale 44, 48, 49
river (drainage) basins 4–5, 12–13, 16, 18, 20
rivers 4–21, 45
rocks 7, 16, 22–3, 44, 48–9; see also limestone
run-off 12, 14–15, 16, 19, 20

science parks 138, 139
sea-level changes 28, 30–1
settlements 64, 80–93, 98–9, 110–11; location factors 84–5, 114
sewage 32, 33, 34–5, 36, 37, 74, 93
shanty settlements 79, 92–3
Shetland 130–1
shops and shopping 89, 94–7, 100, 101, 138, 144–9
soil erosion 21, 74, 126, 156–7
soils 11, 16, 65, 74, 120, 121, 122
South Africa 78–9
spits 26, 27
stacks 23, 48
storm surges 28–9
suburbanised (commuter) villages 86–7

technological development 107–9, 123, 130, 135, 139, 142–3
thermal power stations 132
Tokyo 51, 58–9, 60–1, 75
tourism 107, 140, 150–1, 153, 154–7, 158, 159
transnationals 142, 168–71
transport 65, 74, 86, 90, 91, 94, 96, 98, 100, 101, 103–15, 116, 123, 128, 140
transportation 6, 8–9, 24–5, 38, 42
tsunamis 58, 59

urban growth 16, 86–7, 90–1, 96
urban planning 102–3
urban population 62–3, 74
urban transport 112–13
urbanisation 92–3, 94–103, 110–11, 138
USA 63, 68, 118–19, 134

V-shaped valleys 6, 7
volcanoes 50, 51, 52–7, 60, 61, 64–5, 164–7

water pollution 32–7
waterfalls and gorges 6, 7, 41
watershed 4, 5, 40, 41
wave-cut platforms 22, 26
waves 22–3, 24–5, 26–7
weathering 38, 44
wildlife habitats 150–1, 158–9